# TENANTS

# OF

# THE HOUSE

*(a fictional account of the Nigerian Parliament)*

Wale Okediran

AMV Publishing

AMV Publishing
P.O. Box 661
Princeton NJ 08542-0661
Tel(s): 888-339-6546 (US toll free), 609-5770905 & 732-6476721
Fax: 609-7164770
africarus1@comcast.net & africarus@aol.com

Tenants of the House First US/North American Edition
Copyright © 2011 Wale Okediran

First published in Nigeria in 2009 by
Nelson Publishers Ltd.
Jerich Road, P.M.B. 5164
Ibadan Nigeria

All rights reserved. No part of this publication may be reproduced, stored in a retrieval system, or transmitted in any form or by any means, electronic, mechanical, photocopying, recording or otherwise without the written permission of the Publisher.

Book & Cover Design:
AMV Typographic & Design Unit

Library of Congress Control Number: 2010915329

ISBN:   0-9766941-6-6 (10-Digit)
        978-0-9766941-6-8 (13-Digit)

This is a work of fiction. Parts of it are however based on true events which have been fictionalised. All persons, names, and characters that appear in this book are products of the author's imagination, while the incidents and places mentioned are used fictitiously. Any resemblance to actual events or persons, living or dead is entirely coincidental and exists only in the imagination of the reader.

# DEDICATION

To members of the Fifth session of the Nigerian National Assembly.

# ACKNOWLEDGEMENTS

Heartfelt thanks to my dear wife, Folake, for her usual love and support. To Kola Amodu, sincere thanks for such literary wizardry that turned an otherwise rambling piece of work into an engaging and witty read. Immense gratitude to Maryam Ali, my companion on this literary journey for her sheer poetic brilliance, doggedness and skillful research abilities without which this book would not have been written.

Several good friends such as Femi Osofisan, Tony Marinho, Odia Ofeimun, Tope Olaifa, Denja Abdullahi, James Henshaw Jnr., Amatoritsero Ede, Chika Unigwe, E. C. Osondu, Hon. Sola Adeyeye, Hon. Abike Dabiri-Erewa, Hon. Ade Adegbenjo, Hon. Wole Olakunde, Hon. Usman Bugaje, Hon. John Longhor, Hon. Bakura Lawan among others have been very wonderful with their invaluable contributions.

I will also like to thank my daughters, Ebun, Ore, Seun and Toyin; my secretaries, Glory Kalu-Osong and Moji Atere as well as my publishers for their painstaking editorial and literary input.

Finally, my warm appreciation goes to members of the Abuja Literary Society as well as members of the Abuja and Kaduna Chapters of the Association of Nigerian Authors who were the first recipients of the contents of this book while still in manuscript form. Their important suggestions have enriched the final product.

Why does Mosley always speak to us as though he were a feudal landlord abusing tenants who are in arrears with their rent?

    Clement Attlee (British Prime Minister 1945—51)

# CHAPTER 1

I handled a gun for the first time, the day I saw one in Hon. Elizabeth Bello's handbag. Lizzy and I, both representing Kaduna State, sat next to each other in the chamber of the Federal House of Representatives. She was a smallish, light-complexioned lady, usually dressed in tight-fitting skirt and blouse that accentuated her youthful and enticing thirty-five-year-old body. A single parent with two children, Elizabeth was one of the fifteen women that made up the 360-member parliament.

She had left her seat that day to converse with another Member on the other side of the chamber and urgently needed a document from her handbag, so she asked me to open the bag for her. My heart missed a beat. I swallowed hard. What? I thought; A gun here? You never can tell with women. But there it was, nestled comfortably in a crevice of Lizzy's bag; no nonsense about it, it was the real thing.

I had never handled a gun in my life – until that moment. It was a small light-brown pistol. Elizabeth was brisk and matter-of-fact about it: "Look, Sam," she said. "It is my cute companion. It is small, lightweight and very accurate. Easy to maintain, too."

I found it difficult to think of little Lizzy in her usual tight-fitting outfit as a gun-owner. I had often ogled her youthful and enticing body with male intent. Lizzy's smooth face belied her thirty-five years and her shapeliness did not in any way suggest she was a single parent with two kids.

How had she got the gun, I wondered. She told me an army officer to whom she was very close had given it to her. "It's a Colt Defender. To defend me."

She was amazed to learn that I had never handled a gun in my life.

"Where have you been?" she asked me. "Life is not book, book, book! Get yourself a gun, Sam. Every politician needs one for self-defence."

"Is it loaded?" I asked, stroking the pistol with trepidation.

Lizzy laughed derisively," It's ever-ready."

"But how were you able to beat the metal detectors?" The entrance to our hallowed chambers had metal detectors to scrutinise all incoming traffic, human and non-human.

"How naïve can you get, Sam?" she said. "Look at this." She showed me a lead-lined wallet and then demonstrated how it could be hidden from the metal detector once it was inside the wallet.

"But Lizzy, have you, er, have you, you know, ever had occasion to, em, use this your cute companion?"

"What the ... what kind of question is that? Am I a bumbling starter? You think I am a newcomer to politics like you?" she fairly shouted at me. "Hear this, and hear it well. To kill is a crime: to kill at the right time is politics." For emphasis, she repeated herself in Hausa; "*Kashe mutum laifi ne, amma yin haka a lokacin da ya dace, siyasa kenan!*"

A chill travelled down my spine. I had thought Elizabeth was bluffing in the past about her expertise in politics. But now I remembered that in Kaduna State, where we were both from, her father was a well-known politician. In fact, the family had been in politics for years.

Lizzy had obviously inherited not only her father's natural good looks but also his strength and inde-pendence of mind, traits she needed to survive in the murky waters of the male-dominated world of politics. No party chieftain could browbeat Lizzy; she was direct, combative and hard.

That night, I tossed and turned in bed recollecting the episode of the gun. "To kill is a crime; to kill at the right time is politics." Had Lizzy ever killed anyone? I resolved never to discuss the issue of the gun with her ever again. What did guns have to do with serving one's country? Should I have come to the parliament? Now, I thought, it was too late to go back. The road here was hard. To get my nomination confirmed at the constituency level had been a fierce struggle. I had coughed up half my annual income for the nomination but it was not enough.

"Double the money!" A particularly truculent party chieftain exclaimed. "We know how much you make from your law practice."

I doubled the money but I drew the line at the next outrageous request.

"Meet us at midnight tonight with a newly-made earthenware pot, ten fresh eggs and the drained-out blood of a freshly-killed fowl."

"God forbid!" I screamed. "Give me my money back! A cult – to join a cult! Give me my money back!"

They turned gentle. "Take it easy, Sam. We will use part of the money for the necessary rituals. No cult for you now but you will see the need in future ..."

"I will never see the need. Never bring up the idea again," I screamed with a vehemence that surprised even me.

Perhaps I was naïve. Innocent, I thought, was the better word. I had been in legal practice for a decade; I enjoyed going to court and had done a fair number of cases, making a tidy sum. Politics was something I watched with trepidation and pain. They called it a dirty game but I was a clean man. I would join the game and contribute my quota to good governance and the promotion of a democratic culture.

But I found that most of the dirt in the dirty game was

about money, not merit. Also, the godfathers ignored merit; they were in it for money.

The local party chieftains accepted me for who I was. I survived the long days and sleepless nights and bland repetitive speeches and barely meaningful sloganeering of the endless campaigns. And the money! Every step of the way it was more and more and more money. Money for the chieftains; money for the constituency moguls; money for party stalwarts; money for party thugs; money for the polling agents … I fell asleep and had a dream in which Lizzy said," I will spend three nights with you at the Nicon Noga hotel but you must read this." She then handed me a note, smiling bewitchingly all the time.

The note said,

"Three cosy nights, Barrister Sam, but you must buy me a gun!"

I woke up, screaming, "No!"

\* \* \*

Two years had gone by, two years were left. Should I go through the rigors of a campaign again? Am I not discontented and disillusioned? The thoughts kept coming. Each day was long: from cockcrow to the wee hours of the morning it was debates, meetings, visits, meetings, debates, meetings. I was drained. And I was sadly single. I needed a companion. I remembered the dream and smiled; if I proved strong enough, Lizzy would marry me was my interpretation.

Should I run again? Should I leave the stage now? I moved to my small book collection (oh, how I missed my personal library, a large study in Kaduna) and took down a book. I had underlined the words in red and read them out loud to myself, wondering, pondering. "All political lives, unless they are cut off in midstream at a happy juncture, end in failure, because that is the nature of politics and of human affairs." The words of British rabble-rouser Enoch Powell. Oh, well he had cause to be a pessimist. Never made it to the Prime Ministership. I should choose a happy juncture, I said to myself.

Elizabeth had told me what to do to win future elections. "Fertilizer," she whispered to me urgently, cupping her hands first, then spreading them. "Huge loads of fertilizer is what you need. Money, money, money is the fertilizer of politics. Sam, don't be a small boy. How much do you earn here as a Member of Parliament? Peanuts ... peanuts that godfathers and constituents swallow up as quickly as chickens devour maize."

She paused and spread her dainty hands over the House in a sweeping gesture. "How many Reps make it back? Only two out of ten. Sam, Sam, Sam, and how many times did I call you? You want to make it back? Take the money; make the money, from anywhere, everywhere. Prepare for the rainy day. Politics can be good for you. In this Nigeria, life outside parliament is hard, hard, hard."

She was not done. "Come along Sam," she said and she took me in hand and introduced me to highly influential House Members who would help me to make as much "fertilizer" as possible before that next election.

A week after those introductions, Lizzy introduced me to the Speaker, not by formally intoning his full names and office – Right Honourable Yaya Suleiman, Speaker of the House of Representatives – but simply said, "Yaya, my man, this is Sam. Sam, Yaya is my very close friend."

When I asked Lizzy later what she meant by referring to the Speaker as a very close friend, she told me to mind my own business. "Sam, I have a private life. Don't you forget that. And that is the way it's going to stay."

Her blunt declaration hurt me. I had grown to like Lizzy. She was petite and curvaceous. I had had her to dinner twice but she had not given me signals to go beyond this. I hinted that I was a single parent like her but she was not buying the idea. We were from the same state, I reminded her, and would make a wonderful pair but she merely smiled a thin you-are-not-impressing-me smile.

Agnes had left me four years earlier. I could not find a replacement in Abuja, try as I might. The ladies were there but no relationship lasted. Young and predatory, they sought to milk you for what you were worth. And then they moved on. Only a mature one would settle down, I thought. And Elizabeth was mature enough.

Rumours swirled around Lizzy's name. The soft-sell magazines wrote of her romantic linkages with one Minister and two Senators. But I couldn't care less. I wanted Lizzy. I needed Elizabeth.

One night at ten p.m. Elizabeth's call came. "Come over, Sammy dear. Come quickly!" At last, I said to myself, I have conquered her. I shed my flowing *babbariga*, put on a trendy shirt I had picked up during a recent trip to Havana and doused myself generously with Tomford, my favourite fragrance, then dashed out.

I drove past the Senate President's lodge and noticed an unusual cluster of cars parked in front of it. My mind flashed to ongoing investigations of a bribery allegation against the Senate Chief. Ah, he must be having high-level talks to save his neck, I concluded.

Just before Lizzy's house was the residence of the Deputy Speaker. Parked along the flower-lined driveway were a number of cars, an indication of another political meeting, and a daily routine in the expansive legislator's enclave.

I got to Lizzy's place, shaking my car keys and humming a romantic highlife tune, "Sizzling Lizzy is my girl ... tra la la la ..." I noticed an expensive Mercedes SEC with a Bayelsa State number in her driveway, but it meant little. "Sizzling Lizzy ..." I continued humming.

As I entered the sitting room, a tastefully furnished place, the aroma of a recent smoked cigarette hit my nose. The smoker had to be the man sprawled on the settee. He looked familiar and I searched my mind for his name without success. Then I saw her and my spirits fell. Lizzy was sitting barefoot on the rug at the feet of the smoker. She wore shorts and a halter neck and a half-filled wine glass was cradled in her hand.

Elizabeth, still sitting said, "Sam, this is Honourable Linus Wenike, Member representing Bayelsa State. A very close friend." She patted his thighs seductively and suggestively; my heart missed a beat.

Tall and burly, Linus was a middle-aged man. He wore an expensive, tight-fitting brown silk shirt that accentuated the muscularity of his wide chest. On his neck was a glittering silver chain. My eyes went to his right temple, to a small scar, probably from a knife wound. Linus was impressively, even regally, tall, an imposing figure; but that ugly scar gave no warmth. Worse, his smoking habit had stained his teeth a dirty yellow. He also had a kola nut habit, and those stained teeth put me off. I winced as I shook hands with him.

"Sam, Honourable Samuel Bakura is a new Member from Kaduna State," Elizabeth said waving me to a seat.

"In that case, he is your brother," Linus said, smiling his tobacco-stained smile.

I am more handsome than Lizzy's choice, I thought.

"Yes-o. He's my brother." Lizzy replied," That's why I can trust him to work with us on this project."

What project, I wondered. My mind flew to her comment, "To kill is a crime: to kill at the right time is politics." I hoped nothing murderous was on. The change in my countenance must have registered as both Lizzy and Linus spoke calming words, saying it was a safe project with a handsome reward in view.

"Now Honourable Sam," Linus began. "You are a lawyer. That is a plus. Two, you belong to the opposition party. That is another plus. We have a role for you. You are the man for the role." He reached out for his bag and brought a file out. "These are the project documents. Read them. Study them. And if you have any question, call me."

We exchanged business cards.

I quickly ran my eyes through the documents and immediately understood the nature of the project. Impeachment!

"Lizzy, ah, ah! Why? The Speaker is your friend. Why then do you want him out? I don't get it."

"Yes, Speaker Yaya is my friend. But in this matter he is not. You know the saying, "There are no permanent friends in politics, only permanent interests … *Kar ka kuskura ka bar shi yayi magana."*

I was shaken. Of a truth, I thought, Lizzy was ruthless. She told me, "We have flushed out Yaya. It's just a matter of time. His replacement –" she broke off, searched through an album on a table and brought out a photograph, "– is this handsome man. He will take care of us."

"Yaya is going," she continued. "No two ways about it. There are powerful forces behind our project. The Presidency, Sam, The Presidency is behind us." Suddenly, she clicked her fingers at Linus. "Where is the fertilizer?"

Linus said, "Of course," and fished out an envelope from somewhere. With his crooked smile, he passed to me an immaculate white envelope, whisper-ing, "The first of three instalments."

Quickly, I ripped the envelope open. Many freshly minted American dollars greeted my eyes. "Sizzling Lizzy," I said excitedly, "how much is this?"

Lizzy smiled broadly, her even white teeth a delight for my eyes.

Out of his crooked mouth Linus replied: "Ten thousand dollars."

"It is a deal," I finally said.

# CHAPTER

# 2

It was a wet morning in June. I drove out of the legislators' quarters in Apo. The rain had started before dawn, making it difficult to leave the cosy warmth of my bed. Now, the roads were flooded and the traffic had slowed to a crawl.

As I drove within the sight of the Federal Capital Territory Minister's office at Garki, the rain diminished in intensity. It picked up again as I got to the Federal Secretariat buildings. The rain continued to thrash against the green-domed National Assembly building as I drove past the security personnel at the main gate and into the premises.

Set against a scenic background of rolling hills and quiet ravines, the National Assembly building is a magnificent edifice. On the left shoulder of the sprawling building, painted in the national colours, green and white, are two other symbols of power, the Supreme Court and the Presidential Villa, popularly referred to as Aso Rock.

All three are located in the Maitama District of Abuja, Nigeria's capital. The proximity of the three symbols – representing the executive, legislative and judicial arms of government – gave the area the name Three Arms Zone.

The National Assembly is divided into two chambers, the Senate and the House of Representatives. The Senate is on the left wing; the House of Representatives on the right and has been nicknamed "White House" after the colour of its paint. The building has three floors housing the legislative chambers and office. In the basement are banks, the clinic and offices for support staff.

That day, controversy was in the air and I was filled with anxiety. The hubbub in the House as members gradually filed in did not excite me.

Over and over again I read the sheet of paper in my hand. I was sweating in spite of the air conditioning and my hands were clammy. Suddenly, the mahogany doors of the chamber flew open and the high-pitched voice of the Sergeant-at-Arms rang out in the cavernous hall. "Mr Speaker! Mr Speaker! Mr Speaker!"

In response, Members hitherto chatting in groups moved briskly to their seats, where they remained standing.

The principal officers of the House filed in. Leading them was the Speaker, the Rt. Hon. Yaya Suleiman, from Borno State. Tall, spare and light-complexioned, he looked fresh and radiant. The annual mid-year vacation had done him a lot of good. He was in a cheerful mood and he stopped to share pleasantries with colleagues as he moved to his seat at the head of the chamber. He had no inkling of danger; no idea a plot was afoot to unseat him.

I took yet another look at the sheet of paper in my sweaty hands. Somebody tapped me on the shoulder. It was Honourable Linus Wenike. He looked drawn and surly in spite of his smart wear, the traditional attire of the people of Bayelsa, complete with a hat that hid the knife wound scar.

"Samuel," he whispered "are you set?"

"Of course I am," I replied. "Are the others ready? Where is Bala?"

"Over there, mobilising support," he said, gestur-ing.

Bala, a short bespectacled man in a flowing white *babariga*, was whispering to two Members on the far left side of the chamber.

Linus said, "Bala starts off. If he fails, you will come in. if you fail, we ..."

"Who told you I will fail?" I retorted. "Nobody can stop me today!" I hit my fist on the table.

My fury was interrupted by the opening prayer. The Speaker had reached his seat and was praying.

Almighty God, Ruler of Heaven and Earth, we beseech thee to inspire and guide all our counsel and actions, so that we may always walk in the path of justice, love and charity to one another. Help us unite thy …

With the prayer still on, Lizzy was talking to Hon. Mukter Yinusa. "I … I heard that some Members want to … to … impeach the Speaker!"

Yinusa glanced at her incredulously, smiling, "big joke. Is today April 1? No, no, it can't happen."

Hon. Taiwo Ajayi, Yinusa's neighbour, had overheard the talk. He shook his head vigorously. "Nonsense on stilts!" he said. "Who is the snake, the vile plotter? What has the Speaker done? Nonsense on stilts, I say!"

The Speaker finished the prayer. He moved on to the Notes and Proceedings for the day. Then he went on to the next item on the order paper, the Announcements. He paused in mid-sentence as a commotion in the middle left section of the chamber caught his eye. His voice was stern. "Honourable Bature and Yinusa, please go back to your seats. These announcements are very important."

Lizzy shrugged her shoulders. "Poor Speaker! We are trying to protect him but he does not know it." She then returned to her seat. She had been going round the chamber mobilizing Members against what she considered a sinister attempt to remove the Speaker. The honourable Member Elizabeth Bello, actually one of the conspirators, was playing the role of a decoy. Her part in the whole project was that of a mole in the Speaker's camp.

A hand fell on the nape of her neck. Frowning, turning around and brushing away the intrusive hand, she said, "Who is this …?" Very conscious of her femininity and willowy elegance,

Lizzy, yet wanted to be a politician to be reckoned with. Nobody was going to push her around.

"Sorry, Lizzy. I didn't mean to be rude," the man said.

"Hon. Ajayi, don't dare touch me again, you hear?"

"Sorry, now. I just wanted to say, you should talk to your brother, Hon. Bakura from your state. Tell him to withdraw from this evil plot. It is nonsense and it will fail."

Lizzy shook her head, pushing back a lock of hair from her forehead.

"Hon. Ajayi, Bakura is not the issue. He is a mere player. Do you know the kingpin?"

"Who is he?"

"Hon. Wenike."

"But why?" Ajayi asked.

"Who is the Chairman of the committee of the NDDC?" This is the Niger Delta Development Commission.

"Hon. Ojebode from Ondo State," replied Hon. Ajayi.

"Wenike says he is a more capable person. He says he must become NDDC committee Chairman."

"Is that all? You can't please all the people all the time," Hon. Ajayi said, "That cigarette-smoking so-and-so. Ondo also produces oil. I wonder what kind of Parliament we are. Once you are not given headship of a committee, the next thing is impeachment! Nonsense on stilts!"

"That is not all, Hon. Ajayi. Wenike says the Speaker was bribed," Lizzy said.

"Bribed? No way!" Ajayi replied.

"Wenike says Ojebode paid the Speaker a hundred thousand dollars for the Chairmanship of the NDDC Committee."

"Nonsense on stilts! What is his business with that? Don't mind them? We shall scatter this place today."

"Order, Order!" Cried the Chief Whip, and the agitated chamber began to quieten.

Completely unaware of the brewing plot, the Speaker went on placidly with the day's proceedings. "Honourable Members,

I will now call on Members who have petitions to present to do so."

A few hands went up. "The Speaker recognises Hon. Bala Junaid." Bala, a tall, thickset and corpulent man, rose ponderously to his feet. "Mr. Speaker, my Honourable colleagues, my name is Bala Yahaya Junaid, representing Sokoto Southern Constituency. With your permission, Mr. Speaker, may I sit down?"

Permission granted, Hon. Junaid sat down to present a petition from one of his constituents whose appointment had been wrongly terminated by his employers.

Bala began a long-winded presentation that went on and on. Honourable Elizabeth Bello, Taiwo Ajayi and Muktar Yinusa sidled up to Linus Wenike where he sat with me. Honourable Ajayi spoke first. "Linus, we are colleagues from the last parliament. *Wetin now?* What is this I am hearing?"

Linus growled, "*Leave me bo.* Tribal bigots one and all. You, Ajayi, partnered with the Speaker to give your brother NNPC chairmanship. You have shared out the dollars. A hundred thousand dollar scheme. Shame on you, all. *I beg, leave me-o.*"

"What dollars, Hon. Wenike? What on earth are you talking about? I am no ethnic bigot, let me assure you. I worked for two full years voluntarily in Bayelsa State after my NYSC."

"I can't hear what you are saying. I am not impressed," Linus said.

Yinusa came in. "Committee politics should not be a big deal. The Speaker has the power to appoint committee chairman. House Rule Order VII Section 10(a) and (b) is crystal clear on that. Wenike, you know your House Rules."

"It was sold. No House Rules were applied. Sold! A hundred-thousand-dollar scheme. Shame!" Lizzy and I, who all along had been talking in whispers, began to raise our voices. The Chief Whip interrupted again. "Order! Order! Please Honourable Yinusa, Lizzy, Taiwo and Bakura, go back to your seats."

The members mentioned shuffled to their seats. The chamber soon calmed down.

"Any more petitions?" the Speaker asked.

Bala Junaid's hand went up again.

"Honourable Junaid," the Speaker said, "you have already presented a petition today. I will not therefore allow another from you. Our order paper today is full, please."

Junaid was on his feet in an instant. "With due respect, Mr. Speaker," he said "I have an urgent petition and I wish to present it."

"But if it is urgent why didn't you take it with the previous one?" the Speaker demanded. A murmur of approval rose from his supporters in the Chamber.

Junaid rose again, gesturing wildly. "With due respect Mr. Speaker, no part of our House Rules specifies the order of presentation of petitions. I am free to present my petitions in whatever order as long as they precede the main Orders of the day."

Wenike's group clapped and cheered.

The Speaker gauged the mood of the House. Suddenly a commotion developed. Two members were engaged in a shouting match. The commotion spread to other parts of the chamber. The Speaker raised his voice, seeking to be heard above the noisy exchanges. He could not see why the order of presentation of a petition could trigger uproar. If he allowed Hon. Junaid to have his way he would be thought soft; if he did not he might be thought hard and inflexible. His face did not betray his thoughts. He was still weighing the issue when Hon. Muktar Yinusa went up to him. "Mr. Speaker, refuse Junaid I say. He is an ant to finish you. It is a side plan. They want to impeach you. It is a side plan to weaken you before they bring up the issue of impeachment." To drive home his point, Muktar repeated himself in Hausa; *"Kar ka kuskura ka bar shi yayi magana."*

The Speaker grew suddenly dizzy. "Im ... peachment?" A big joke!"

"Wenike is behind it. He has stirred up trouble against you. Bala ... he wants to use Bala to test his group's strength. Stop Bala!"

Lizzy and Taiwo ran up to the Speaker's seat to advise him.

"Order! Order!" The Chief Whip's cry went unheeded. It took all of five minutes for the Speaker to calm members down.

As the commotion subsided, the Speaker grew tense. He was unsure how to proceed. He decided to gamble. Let the chips fall where they may, he muttered to himself. "Honourable, Bala Junaid you may now present your petition."

The Wenike group roared in approval. Bala had set the ball rolling. It was my turn. Meanwhile, Linus Wenike was in a tête-à-tête with Hon. Lamidi Kasali, the tough godson of a tough godfather from Oyo State. Kasali, a tall hefty fellow whose one qualification for his parliament seat was his unalloyed loyalty to his crusty godfather, was a former chairman of the drivers' and conductors' union. A real roughneck, Kasali was a veteran of bare-knuckle fights in the streets of Ibadan.

"We are grabbing the mace," Wenike told Kasali. "I will throw it to you. Catch it and make a dash for the door ..."

"Which door, the main door?" Kasali asked, squinting with alcohol-soaked eyes in the direction of the mace where it lay on its table directly in front of the Speaker's seat.

"No, Kasali, not the main door, the door behind the Speaker. A member of the chamber has opened it, just for us. Dash out of that door. Outside, my PA and driver will receive the mace and run with it. *Shikena!*"

"No fertilizer?"

"Ha, Hon. Kasali. My word is my bond. I will ...

"I want it now or never!" Kasali insisted.

Stealing the mace would cripple the house. With the mace, the symbol of authority, in our hands, our impeachment plan would be eighty percent successful.

Hon. Bala Junaid had finally concluded his deliberately protracted presentation.

Relieved that he had done with the troublesome lawmaker, the Speaker switched on his microphone. "The first Order of the

Day is a Motion on the conduct of the Nigerian Police Force, standing in the name of Hon …"

"Point of Order, Mr. Speaker," I bellowed into the microphone.

Some Members were irritated at the interruption. Others were excited.

The Speaker, a seasoned politician, was caught off guard. Should he allow the Point of Order or not? Was I part of Wenike's group or not? Was I for or against the impeachment plot? As Speaker Suileman pursed his lips in thought, an ominous silence descended on the Chamber. "Order what?" the Speaker heard himself say seconds later.

"Order V, subsection 2 on page II of the House Rules," I said, my heart pounding with excitement.

"What does it say?"

I rose to my feet. "Mr. Speaker, Honourable Members, my name is Samuel Bakura. I represent Kaduna South Constituency. Order V subsection 2 states that 'Any member may rise at any time to speak upon a matter of privilege suddenly arising' …"

"No! No! No!" came the chorus from the Speaker's supporters. They had suddenly realised that Bakura was about to throw a bomb!

The Wenike group began to shout down the Speaker's group. The House was engulfed in prolonged uproar for ten minutes. The upshot: I was allowed to take the floor. My nervousness had disappeared. A fresh and unusual courage coursed through my veins. "Mr. Speaker, having been given the permission as contained in Order V, subsection 2 to speak on a matter of privilege, I wish to straight away ask the Honourable Speaker to invoke subsection 3 of the same Order and suspend all other business until my matter has been heard and …"

The Speaker came in. "Honourable Bakura, you have not informed us of the matter you are raising for debate. Without that, one cannot establish a prime facie case of breach of privilege as stated in the same subsection 3 which you have just quoted. I therefore advise you to tell this honourable Chamber the matter you want to talk about."

Far from being flustered by this minor setback, I became bolder. My speech, I noticed, was already troubling the Speaker, who sat hunched and tired in his chair, staring ahead, stunned and suspicious.

I went on. "Honourable Speaker, my matter has to do with the recent change in the appointment of Committee Chairmen which …"

The Speaker's supporters raised a chorus: "No! No! No!"

The Wenike group answered the chorus: "Yes! Yes! Yes!"

The uproar spread through the Chamber. Voices were raised in angry debate.

The Speaker beckoned to the House Leader, Hon. Musa Muritala, and confessed his confused state of mind to his friend in Hausa. *"Kai Duk na rude, me zan yi ne ma?"*

The short distraction was all that Wenike needed. He walked towards the Speaker's seat as if he was going to confer with him, then suddenly lunged towards the mace, snatching it in an instant and yanking it off its base. He flung it to Hon. Kasali, who caught it deftly and sprinted with it through the rear door. The Sergeant-at-Arms and his staff were helpless. As they futilely rushed out after Kasali, Lizzy took her mobile phone out of her bag, switched it on and dialled the President's number. After the call, she brought her mirror from her bag and began to adjust her lipstick.

# CHAPTER 3

Kayode Smollet was in high spirits as he entered his office in the basement of the House that June afternoon. A former Senator, he had been made the President's point man in the often turbulent House of Representatives because of his legislative experience and contacts. His official designation was Presidential Liaison Officer to the House of Representatives.

He was in high spirits because he had coordinated part of the events that led to the disappearance of the mace from the Chambers of the House of Representatives. The middle-aged man from Osun in the South-West was thrilled at the success of his first major assignment in the parliament. He was also exhilarated that he would make a tidy sum from the scheme. For the former Senator, the position was a plum one. His new salary was more than double his old one.

He now pondered his next line of action. Would the President accede to his plan, he wondered. Presently, his driver arrived to take him to the Presidential Villa. As he was about to enter his car, Senator Smollet saw the newshounds and braced himself for inquiries. The journalists were clustered in the lobby and they swarmed around him eagerly.

"Senator, we learnt you are to brief the President …"

"Is it true that the Presidency is behind the Speaker's attempted impeachment?"

"Is it true you have custody of the mace?"

"What will be the President's next line of action?"

Senator Smollet had a sharp one-line answer for each highly excited question. Finally he was able to extricate himself from the journalists.

He wondered how they knew he was on his way to the Villa. He knew his driver – also his cousin, and a talkative one at that – was possibly the culprit. He suddenly brought up the issue. "Muri, how did those journalists know where I was going?"

"I am not the one, sir. I did not tell them anything."

"Don't tell me that. You are always not the one. The same thing happened the last time I was to travel with the President to Osogbo."

"*Walahi*, oga, it wasn't me. Which journalist do I know? I don't even read the newspaper."

"You are lying, Muri. You are always with them at the joint, drinking."

"Only Brother Marcus. Only Brother Marcus of *The Clarion*. No one else ..."

"Anyway, next time I will give you a red card. This is the last warning. *Clarion* or no *Clarion*, let this be the last time journalists will harass me. If it happens again, back to Osogbo you go to your 'Okada' business. My job is sensitive. Confidential ... It demands a lot of confidentiality, Muri, enh ... *se oti gbo*?"

"Yes sir."

Finally, they drove up to the Villa. President Ambrose Oneya had heard the news of the stolen mace even before the Head of the State Security Service informed him. He saw Smollet come up just as he was about to leave his office for the Executive Chamber for the meeting of the Executive Council. The President decided to delay the meeting until he had been fully briefed by his Liaison Officer in the National Assembly.

Smollet found the President pacing about restlessly in his office. The President, a middle-aged man from Delta State, sat down to listen to Smollet and exploded at the end of the Senator's account.

"What? Those bloody fools! They've done it again! The mace, the mace ... why steal the mace? Just get rid of the damn fellow. What's difficult about that?"

"Your Excellency, it was a very tough session ..." the former Senator began.

The President interrupted him, "Of course. I know it was bound to be difficult. Tough tasks for tough men. That's why I put you there. Or is the little job of getting rid of the Speaker too much for you, Senator Smollet? Speak and let me hear you."

"Your Excellency, we shall remove him. It was just that Wenike's supporters were so determined."

"Were you, Honourable – I mean Senator – Smollet, part of the scheme to steal the mace?"

"Believe me, Your Excellency, it was the only way out. Speaker Suileman has many friends in the House. The man is grounded, well grounded. But we shall shake him and flush him out. Conventional tactics will fail. Unorthodox measures ..."

The President's Principal Secretary emerged to tell him the minutes were all ready for the council meeting.

"Go on, Kayode. How will stealing the mace help our cause?"

"Your Excellency, the absence of the mace has put the Speaker and his group on the defensive. The whole nation knows that the mace is the symbol of the authority of the House. If they don't do our will, we can form a parallel House."

"But you can't do that, Smollet. How will you get the required two-thirds of your members?"

"It has been done before, your Excellency. Fertilizer! We shall spread the muck and woo enough Members to our side."

"I want this done quickly. Wooing and mucking ... how long will that take us?"

"Your Excellency, we shall make haste. But we need to proceed gradually if we want to succeed. Acting too fast may jeopardise our plans. Two weeks, give us two weeks to woo them – if we have enough funds, that is."

"Two weeks?"

"Your Excellency, two weeks."

The President's face lit up in a smile for the first time since the discussion began. "Great! Two weeks is great," he said with a chuckle. "How much will you need?"

Smollet smacked his lips, his eyes glinting with satisfaction. He fished out a calculator from somewhere, pressed some buttons and moments later wrote out the final figure for the President.

The President spoke. "No, that is way too much. I am sure if we offer the damned fellow half the sum, he will willingly leave the seat."

Smollet laughed heartily. "Your Excellency, success costs money. The strategy is pure and simple: hit them, hit them hard; give them what they dare not reject. Sir, we must remember it is a contest of wills and resources. It's a tug of war: naira for naira, dollar for dollar. Money is the name of the game; Your Excellency."

President Oneya fell into deep thought, his head bowed. After a full two minutes, he rose, glanced at his wristwatch and dismissed Smollet. "OK, I will ask Desmond to get the money ready. Of course, I will reduce it by thirty per cent …"

"Make it twenty per cent, your Excellency. The media boys must have their own envelopes. Without a compliant media, the project may fail."

*"Hmn. Hmn.* OK, Desmond will see you tomorrow."

One more thing, your Excellency."

The President raised a quizzical brow. "Yes?"

"The information aspect. We must bug the Speaker's office and official quarters, as I told you before."

"Is that necessary?"

"We must be ahead of them all the time, your Excellency."

The President paused for a while, thinking hard. "No messy

operations, please. Remember Watergate and Nixon's fall. Are you sure your idea will not hurt our case?"

"It will help our case, President. Our security agents are experts. The information gathered will help us tremendously."

The President paused again. He then pressed a bell. His ADC entered, saluting smartly.

"Get me Yakubu," the President ordered.

Moments later Lieutenant Colonel Yakubu emerged.

"Yes, Yakubu. Senator here has a little job for you. See him. Do a neat job, OK?"

"Yes, sir!"

"Use your best men! No leakages, no mistakes, you understand?"

"Yes, sir!

With that the President opened the door and surrounded by his aides sauntered into the council chamber.

"I don't know how you could have missed a plot of this magnitude. Were you all sleeping? In politics you sleep with one eye open." This was Speaker Yaya Suleiman. He was in a sour mood. He was uncomfortable and in spite of the air conditioning, beads of sweat stood out on his forehead.

He faced the Chief Whip. "It beats me hollow. I mean, none of our boys got wind of the wicked plot. What are we going to do now?" He threw his hands round the room expansively as he asked the last question. The principal officers were there, as was Hon. Elizabeth Bello.

The House leader, a corpulent ex-secondary school principal, sighed deeply, staring into space. "Let us give it to them: it was a well-planned operation. Only God knows how they beat us to it," he added.

"Money," the Chief Whip interjected, "money is what they used."

"Hurray! Hurray for us!" said the Deputy Leader. "If it is a matter of money, they are finished; we shall outspend them."

The House Leader spoke again. "Not basically, money,

gentlemen. Let us face it: our intelligence and information-gathering methods failed us. They are rusty. We need to invest more in espionage."

"Espionage? James Bond stuff. *Tufia*. Not on your life. This is politics, not war," said the Chief Whip.

"It is war, my friend," the Deputy Leader pointed out. "According to the great war theorist Karl von Clausewitz, politics is war carried out by other means."

None of the other Members had ever heard of Clausewitz. They all looked blank for a moment.

The Deputy said, "The Leader is right. We need to eavesdrop on their conversations and meetings and get-togethers and the best way to do so is to infiltrate their ranks ..."

"But where is the mace?" the Speaker asked.

The Leader said, "It must be here in Abuja."

"But where, where, precisely where? I would hate for them to organize a parallel sitting."

"You are right, Mr. Speaker," the Leader replied, "we must not be caught with our trousers down. In the last House the mace was stolen, a parallel sitting was organized and then the Speaker was impeached. Mr. Speaker, we have to tread the path of diplomacy. Befriend them. Woo them. Force will not work. Fighting them will not be in our interest."

The Chief Whip, an ex-sergeant rumoured to have been discharged from the army for embezzling soldiers' salaries, interjected with passion. "Clausewitch, or whatever his name is, would not agree. Politics is war. War is politics. Fire for fire! A soldier is a soldier. We won't beg anybody – *kar mu ragama 'yan, banzan!*"

"Clausewitz is his name. Chief Whip, you know now, war is not a singularity. The nature of war changes: different battles, different tactics. Sometimes you advance on the enemy; sometimes you talk with the enemy. According to the great Karl von Clausewitz ..."

"I'm sorry, DL," the Speaker butted in. "We need to move forward. Practical suggestions! Practical steps! Enough of your old school philosophy. In the next twenty-four hours, what should be our agenda?"

Lizzy had been silent all the while. The Speaker had co-opted her into the meeting, assuming she was a loyalist. However, Lizzy was indeed the spearhead of the impeachment plot. In her handbag was her pistol, the ever-ready Colt Defender, and a small tape recorder taking down every word spoken that evening.

The meeting came to a consensus: the Speaker and the other principal officers were to meet the ringleaders of the opposition in an attempt to placate them.

The Chief Whip raised the issue of propaganda. "We shall use the media. I will call a press conference to sell the dummy. I will give the impression that some members of the Wenike group have switched sides to us."

"Who are the main sponsors of the impeachment?" asked the Leader. "We need to know them. Remember that the President has complained on several occasions that we are not a co-operative House. My hunch is that Oneya does not trust Mr. Speaker and he wants to replace him with a stooge."

"No need to beat about the bush, then. The President is behind the impeachment move," said the Chief Whip. "In fact, someone once stumbled on a meeting between Senator Smollet and Hon. Wenike and his group planning something."

Lizzy spoke for the first time. "Who is Senator Smollet?"

"He is from Osun State. The PLO," the Speaker said. PLO was the well-known abbreviation for the Presidential Liaison Officer at the National Assembly.

"When was he seen?" the Leader asked.

"About a fortnight ago, I got the information but it meant nothing to me then. Looking back, the plan has been on for a long time."

"In that case," the Leader observed, "we have a battle ahead of us, a long and difficult battle. We shall attack on several fronts. Name it – diplomacy; name it – intrigue; name it – blackmail; name it – propaganda. Mr. Speaker, we must move fast. We are on the defensive, you see, they have the mace. We need to move before they organise a parallel sitting. And Mr. Speaker, we need money. If the President is truly the brain behind the plot, we are in serious trouble. How can we match the Presidency naira for naira, dollar for dollar?"

The Honourable Speaker bowed his head sadly, his mood gloomy.

The Chief Whip spoke. "All is not lost. Let us not lose hope. The diplomats are there, the civil society, the media. We can influence public opinion. But fast. We must move fast."

An idea began to take shape in the Speaker's mind. The more he thought of it, the more workable it seemed. After allowing the Chief Whip and the other Principal Officers to talk some more, he took a sip of water, cleared his throat and said, "As the Leader said, we must move on all fronts. This is how it will go. Leader, you will lead the team that will tackle the journalists; the Chief Whip will deal with the diplomatic corps. The Deputy Speaker and I will go to the Presidency. The Deputy Leader will speak with Wenike. You are close to him, are you not? Lizzy is even closer, the two of you will work on Wenike …"

"Excuse me Mr. Speaker," the Chief Whip suddenly said. "*Bari in bayyana maka wani abu muhimmi a nan* … I have an important point to make,"

"Yes?"

"We must not forget House Members, the undecided majority, so that they can flock to our side."

"No," the Deputy Leader said. "They are sure to support us."

The Speaker came in. "The Chief Whip has a point. We need to lobby the fence-sitters. Don't take anyone for granted, please. In fact, we have to work on those already on our side. We must watch our backs. Many more politicians have been destroyed by their supporters than by their opponents. Well, Deputy Whip, please take up that role."

The Speaker spoke the final words: "Each group has to report back in forty-eight hours. The clock starts ticking now. I will call the Villa to book an appointment to see the President. As soon as I get the signal, I will ask the Deputy Speaker and a few other members to go with me."

# CHAPTER 4

The rain started again towards the evening when most people were home relaxing after a hectic day's work. Initially a drizzle, the late evening shower soon turned into another heavy downpour. At the security post of the National Assembly, the four policemen on duty took advantage of the rain to put out the lights in their office, arrange the cushions on the chairs together and stretch out comfortably for the night.

It was only the State Security Service officer who still remained glued to the television, on the pretext that he wanted to watch a late-night movie. However, on the dot of ten o'clock, he used his mobile phone to alert his other colleagues waiting in a dark Range Rover parked discreetly at the back entrance of the White House.

Three men emerged surreptitiously from the van, each carrying two shoebox-sized cartons. The leader, an officer of the State Security Service selected a key from a large bunch that he produced from his pocket and used it to open the back door.

Once in the deserted and poorly-lit lobby of the White House, the group moved towards the Speaker's office. In the corridor adjoining the office, the leader used a ladder already stationed beside the wall to climb to the ceiling. He remove three of the white plastic ceiling tiles; one after the other, the three men climbed into the roof and were presently in the Speaker's office. With the aid of a wood chisel, three recesses, each about two inches square, were made, one in the wood panel directly behind the Speaker's desk, one under the Chief of Staff's desk and one in the secretary's table.

Three radio transmitters each complete with its own miniature power pack were extracted from the cartons. They were quickly snuggled neatly into the recesses and covered with plasticine the colour of the wooden panels.

Having completed their mission, the three men left as discreetly as they came. Taking the staircases two at a time, they were soon in the basement of the building where they installed the custom-built receiver and the voice-activated tape recorder tuned to the wavelength of the transmitter. Glad at the success of the operation, one of the officers, obviously eager for more action, asked, "When are we going to bug his house?"

"Not tonight, but definitely very soon," came the reply.

The Dorchester was one of those new state-of-the art hotels that dotted the Abuja landscape like pimples on an adolescent's face. Tucked away in a corner of Wuse Zone 4, the two-storey building was aglow with merriment that June evening. In the "Tropical Hall" section, Hon. Linus Wenike and our group were meeting. It was our first meeting since the mace had been successfully snatched from the House of Representatives chamber.

In attendance were key members of the group: Hon. Elizabeth Bello, Honourable Samuel Bakura (me), Hon. Lanre Kasali, Hon. Muktar Yinusa, Hon. Taiwo Ajayi and Hon. Bala Junaid. With us were members who, excited and impressed by what had happened earlier in the chamber, had decided to join the group. Among them were three female members who all sat with Lizzy in a corner of the hall.

Looking through the hotel window, I was sad to see that it had started raining again. I needed good weather to enable me to keep a date later on with one pretty nurse that I had met in the NASS clinic where I had gone to check my blood pressure earlier. The rain, however, did not take anything from the joy and celebration that was going on in the room. We were all in a happy mood as we all clapped and sang along with the music that was blaring out of a loudspeaker. Meanwhile bottles of Cristal, Courvoisier and other expensive drinks were being opened one after the other and the contents generously gulped with careless abandon. In one corner of the hall, I caught a glimpse of Lizzy dancing with a tall member from Edo State. Both were in high spirits, judging from the way they gyrated to the music.

Suddenly Hon. Linus Wenike entered the hall and the crowd cheered, "Leader! Leader! Leader!" as he went on to sit on the small podium where two chairs had been set. He was closely followed by Hon. Kasali, who now acted as his unofficial ADC. Another familiar figure whose name I could not recollect sat in the second one.

"Well done everybody, well done!" Linus started. He introduced the man in the second chair as Senator Kayode Smollet, a former senator and current Presidential Liaison Officer in the National Assembly. "Senator Smollet has a message for us from the Presidency and I want all of us to listen attentively."

Just then, Hon. Bala Junaid observed that we should make sure that there were no spies among us before the Senator passed on very sensitive information; but he was overruled by Hon. Ajayi. "I don't think we should worry about that. We have nothing to hide now. Every Nigerian knows that we intend to get rid of the Speaker. The demand that he reconstitutes the Chairmanship of the Committees is just a ploy to box him in a corner. The only news we need to hide is the location of the mace; and that will remain secret for as long as this fight continues."

Hon. Ajayi's speech was greeted with cheers by everybody, after which the Senator took the floor. The gist of his speech was that the Presidency was fully behind us in our quest to install a Speaker who could generate the confidence required of a good leader. He ended his speech by handing over a "Ghana-must-go" bag to Linus for onward distribution to Members of the group. This last act generated a loud ovation among the group.

After Senator Smollet had been excused, Hon. Wenike told our group of the Speaker's intention to hold a dialogue with our group through the Deputy Leader and Lizzy. He asked whether or not the group was ready for dialogue with the Speaker. A resounding No! No No! greeted his speech. "We don't want it, we don't want it, we don't want it!" came the chant.

Hon. Muktar Yinusa felt that it was too early for dialogue with the Speaker and insisted that the only credible choice left was for him to step down.

"Instead of an outright removal, can't we just force him to readjust the chairmanship positions so that we can get juicy positions for members of our group?" asked Hon. Taiwo Ajayi.

However, Hon. Linus Wenike pointed out that what our sponsors wanted was a new Speaker and not chairmanship positions. "Our brief from the presidency is to effect a change of Speaker. And since the incoming Speaker is our man who has promised to take good care of us we would end up killing two birds with one stone."

However, I reminded the meeting that we had no concrete evidence against the Speaker to warrant his impeachment. "Don't forget that Section 5 subsections (i) and (iii) of the constitution is very clear on the conditions that must be met before a Speaker can be impeached." I added.

"You are the lawyer. Tell us exactly what the constitution says,"Linus said.

From my hip pocket, I brought out a small copy of the constitution from where I read the relevant part. The exposition generated a lot of debate on whether or not we had sufficient grounds with which to impeach the Speaker. While some members such as Hon. Kasali suggested that we could go ahead and fabricate some 'sins' against the Speaker, Hon. Wenike observed that the term 'found guilty of acts inimical to the interests of the House in the constitutional provision for impeachment' was enough cover for us.

As he put it, "Any act, from not giving us enough funds to

blocking our other opportunities for improvement, gives enough grounds for impeachment. Therefore, I believe that a lopsided committee chairmanship arrangement is enough."

"In addition to this, once we can confirm the allegation of the $100,000 bribe from Hon. Ojebode, then we are home and dry," Lizzy commented as she sipped from a glass of wine, her beautiful hair now in a ponytail. I could still feel some stirring in me as I ogled her in a lowcut cream blouse that revealed some of her enchanting fair skin, glistening so beautifully under the fluorescent lights of the hotel hall.

I managed to tear my eyes away from her as I quickly reminded the group of our next hurdle. "Now, we have to muster the required two-thirds majority that the constitution stipulates for the impeachment."

"That is easy," shouted Lizzy.

"No, it's not," Hon. Yinusa objected. "Dont forget that the Speaker and his group also have their own sponsors."

"So what? They can't match us naira for naira, dollar for dollar," said Lizzy, her high-pitched voice indicating that she was slightly tipsy. Her reaction soon generated another round of argument that before long degenerated into an uproar. While one group believed that getting a two-thirds majority was no problem, the other group felt otherwise. As the argument see-sawed each way, I decided to be a bit scientific. I did a quick headcount and discovered that there were only 30 of us in the room. I managed to raise my voice above the din of voices to let them know our real strength.

"Two-thirds of 360 is 240, which means we still have a long way to go," I pointed out, then advised them on the way forward.

"If we are really serious about this impeachment plan, I advise that we set up a small committee to get more members on our side. It will be better if we do this on a geopolitical basis, two members each to cover each zone with the mandate to get about 60 members per zone within a deadline. This is the only way by which we can achieve our objective. With anything short of this, our impeachment plan can never work."

As I said this, all was quiet for a while. Obviously, the group had never figured that the "project" would be that difficult. As the reality of my statement hit them, the hitherto ebullient group quietened down. It was Linus who spoke first. "Samuel, what deadline do you have in mind?' he asked.

"Since impeachment is mainly political, we need to move fast. Seven days is the best we have."

"Seven days?" Taiwo Ajayi said. "How can we mobilise over 200 members within seven days?"

"It's possible if we really mean business," Linus said.

"What it means is that we have to distribute the work among ourselves tonight and meet again for feedback in the next three days."

Again, the hall became quiet.

Muktar Yinusa was the first to speak. "My dear colleagues, I think we need to take another look at this project. When we first started, I was made to understand that it had to do with the appointment of committee chairmen. I thought that if the Speaker were threatened he would reconsider the appointments he had made so that those of us who were aggrieved can be taken care of. From what has happened today, it is obvious that we have been able to put him on the defensive. I think we should now use our advantage to bargain with him for better deals and not to totally impeach him. I am an old Member of the House and I can say with all sense of responsibility that impeachment is not all that easy. First, how do we mobilise 240 members within a few days? Second, where are we going to get the resources, knowing fully well that the Speaker and his group also have their own sponsors? Assuming that the Presidency is on our side, how much can we get from that end knowing well how stingy the President is? Third, do we know how rich the Speaker's war chest is? My own advice is that we should force the Speaker to take care of us through the reconstitution of the Chairmen of the

Committee and forget about the impeachment exercise."

Four other Members spoke after Muktar. Three supported the idea of impeachment, while the fourth spoke against the plan. "For effective mobilisation of members, we shall need about N500,000 per member, making a total of N120 million for 240 of them," said the fourth speaker, a short thickset Member from Imo State. "This is apart from the money we have to spend on publicity and the media. You will therefore agree with me that we need a lot of money which we might find difficult to gather."

It was getting close to midnight when Linus finally rounded up the meeting. As I had expected, he admonished us to go on with the plan and not to allow the issue of how to get the money to distract us.

"I don't know who told Hon. Muktar that the exercise was just to have the Speaker reschedule the committee chairmanship appointments. At no time did we discuss such an issue. The brief I had from the word go was to impeach the Speaker and that is what we shall do. Mobilising members for the task may appear difficult; but by the time we start the propaganda war, I can assure you that we shall get the required number of Members within the next three days. We won't even spend a quarter of the figure that Muktar has projected. So, my dear colleagues, I want you all to be steadfast and rest assured that our project is doable. We shall spend the few minutes remaining for this meeting to give out duties to everybody. Apart from those who will mobilise Members, some of us will have to work with the media while others will need to link up with some state governors who will assist us in getting Members from their states on our side. More importantly, we need to get more sponsors so that we can match our opponents, naira for naira, dollar for dollar. I will therefore appreciate it if those of you with contacts can come up with names of potential sponsors. We also need those with contacts with the press."

Linus thereafter appointed the two Members per geopolitical zone to mobilise more Members for the group. In spite of my protests, I was paired with another member from Niger state for the North-Central zone. This was in addition to my other roles in the impeachment saga.

Linus was still in the middle of this arrangement when the issue of the whereabouts of the mace came up. He assured the house that the mace was safe, but said that for strategic reasons its whereabouts as well as our next line of action would not be discussed for now, these things will be discreetly disclosed in the next 24 hours. We were about rounding off when Hon. Okey Azika from Enugu state raised his hand up to speak.

"What about the gift from the Presidency? I think its important that we should share this before we depart."

As you would expect, his statement generated another uproar. Some members agreed with him, maintaining that the money would encourage members to continue the struggle; but a sizeable number did not want the money to be shared.

"We need to keep the money for very important logistical arrangements that definitely lie ahead," observed Lizzy. However, Okey maintained his position and was soon supported by members that included the very influential Hon. Muktar.

In the end, Linus had no choice but to agree to share the money with the stipulation that he would keep about twenty per cent of it for unforeseen expenses.

"The total sum here is forty million naira. It is the first instalment of what is to come, so, let's just manage it," Linus said as he handed a million naira (about eight thousand US dollars) to each of us.

And just as we predicted, the money raised the morale of members as Linus assured them that more money was on the way. "Everybody should therefore perform his duties to the best of his ability. I can assure you that victory will certainly be ours at the end of the day," he added, to cheers of "Leader! Leader! Leader!"

More drinks were served, after which the D.J. put on P-Square's famous piece "This Game Is Over", which was then top of the country's music chart. We all trooped to the dance floor chanting the song's chorus.

"This game is over, I know it, you know it, we know, we know it. Eh– eh-eh! Oh – oh-oh!

I soon managed to sidle up to Lizzy with whom I soon engaged in a hearty and energetic dance as we both sang the song.

*If I dey go look left*
*make you dey look right*
*if I dey look up*
*make you dey look down*
*pack up and leave*
*carry dey go*
*waka dey go*
*I am telling you, this game is over*
*Eh- eh-eh! Oh- oh-oh!*
*I know it, you know it, we know it.*

# CHAPTER 5

It had been a difficult day for the Speaker of the Federal House of Representatives. Almost all the reports that came back to him from the different groups he had sent out were negative. All his entreaties to the Wenike group had been rebuffed, while his other plans on how to tackle his opponents had collapsed even before they took off. It was as if a spy had been recording every speech and every movement from his camp. To make matters worse, the much-awaited meeting with the President had not taken place, with the Chief of Staff claiming that the President was very busy. Even his calls to the President's hotline were being ignored.

His worst nightmare came when it was discovered that members of his group had started moving to the Wenike group to whom the Presidency had reportedly given the hefty sum of N100 million to effect his removal. When, in desperation, he had got in touch with the banks and corporate organisations that normally did business with the House, all he received were promises but no concrete answers.

He kept pacing up and down the small office attached to his official residence at the zone E Section of the Apo Legislators Quarters hours after his family had gone to bed. He slowly sipped a can of cold beer as he went over the events of the past 48 hours. He was especially flustered that he never got wind of any of the opposition's plans before then as he normally did in the past. As a senior member of the ruling Total Democratic Party, he could not remember when and how he had offended the President so much so that he would want him out of office. He could also not recollect having offended the Party's Chairman, officials or even his State's Governor; as a result, he did not understand what could have caused the persecution he was now experiencing.

Going over all this, the Rt. Hon. Yaya Suleiman's mood got gloomier. To calm himself down, he took a pipe from the windowsill. Patiently, he filled the bowl from a tobacco pouch, taping down the fresh tobacco with his thumb. He struck a match, an action which in the stillness of the empty office sounded as loud as a firecracker coming to life.

Hon. Yaya drew on the pipe stem as the smoke began to rise until the tobacco became well alight like the bellows at a blacksmiths. He puffed the blue smoke into the air and lazily watched the cloud like a haze ascend the low ceiling. As he relaxed in the warmth of the smoke, the literary enthusiast reached to the adjoining bookshelf as his eyes went through an array of books.

His gaze soon fell on his favourite poet, Rabindranath Tagore, the great Indian poet who was awarded the Nobel Prize in 1913 for his outstanding book *Gitanjali*. He leafed through the book, needing to do something to lift his spirits. Suddenly his eye caught a thought-provoking piece: "This is my prayer to thee, my Lord."

*This is my prayer to thee, my Lord – strike, strike at the root of penury in my heart, give me the strength lightly to bear my joys and sorrows. Give me the strength to make my love fruitful in service. Give me the strength never to disown the poor or bend my knees before insolent might. Give me the strength to raise my mind high above daily trifles. And give me the strength to surrender my strength to thy will with love.*

As he went from page to page, his spirit lifted and the weariness of his mind soon dissolved to be replaced by a soothing feeling of peace, calm and hope. Now that he could think better, he decided to fight back. He would need to tackle his opponents one by one. He would attempt to unbalance the big ones by tackling the small ones, those that made up their Achilles' tendon. As he thought of this new idea, he smiled to himself. He knew he had to start straight away for time was not his friend.

He opened a safe behind his seat and brought out some naira notes. Working quickly, he put the equivalent of 2,000 dollars each into ten brown envelopes and packed them into a bag. He collected a car key from the table, called Usman, his Personal Assistant, and said; "*zo mu tafi, wani al'amari na gaggawa ya taso* … please, lets go for an urgent mission." He drove out of the compound in a light-blue BMW. It was two in the morning.

I was roused from sleep by the persistent ringing of the doorbell that seemed to be coming from afar. Now as I sleepily rubbed my eyes and peered through the bedroom window into the well lit drive in, I wasn't sure whom I was looking at. I was still wondering if I was dreaming when the familiar voice called out. "Hon. Samuel, its me the Speaker. Kindly come and open the door."

For a brief moment, my mind was in turmoil. I was scared of being seen with the Speaker in my house at this time of night. I didn't want to appear as a sellout; at the same time, I couldn't leave the Speaker, the fourth most powerful person in the country, out in the dark on my doorstep. Courtesy demanded that I attended to him.

I was soon at the doorstep, and found the Speaker standing alone, in a loose-fitting grey shirt over black trousers. Despite the turmoil of the past few days he appeared relaxed and calm as a small smile played on his lips.

"I am awfully sorry Honourable for getting you up so late," he said.

"No Honourable Speaker, I am the one who should apologise for keeping you waiting. I slept very late and – you, er, didn't have to come, sir. All you needed to do was call me to come to you, sir," I replied as I led him into the sitting room.

"I know it's late sir, but can I offer you something?" I asked.

"Its okay, Honourable. Although it's late, as it's my first time in your house, I will take something. Let me have a Martini with ice."

I was very nervous as I mixed the drinks in my kitchen. I was like a rat facing a trap. Whichever way my encounter with the Speaker went, I was sure that my credibility would still be at stake. Suddenly an idea came to my mind: quickly I eased out my latest Prada Blackberry from my bag and flicked on the recording device. I replaced it in my front shirt pocket where it could easily pick up voices.

Back in the sitting room, I handed the drink over to the Speaker while I nursed mine.

The Speaker took a swig, cleared his throat, leant forward and said, "My dear Honourable, when I first saw your CV on the National Assembly website, I was happy that I had a colleague with whom I could move this our fledging democracy forward. As you are aware, we all came into this National Assembly from different backgrounds and with different intentions. While some of us like you and me are well-educated, we have others who are not. And while some came here with altruistic intentions, others came only to feather their nests, and they will do anything to achieve this purpose. As a lawyer myself, a senior one for that matter, my plan was to utilise the expertise of my learned colleagues such as you to try to educate our other colleagues on how to steer this democracy in the path of maturity to a level we can all be proud of. Unfortunately, as a Member of the opposition, I could not make you the chairman of any committee and that's why it appeared that I have neglected you. Despite this, I know that with your brains, charisma and drive, there are other important duties I can saddle you with. There are very important bills, motions and legislative activities which you can help to organise."

He paused to take another drink.

"I cannot but shudder at the quality of the kind of people you are associating with in that your group. With due respect to them, I still believe that you are superior in educational and moral background and should normally not be conniving with the likes of Wenike, Lasisi and Muktar to unseat me. These are people who barely passed their O-levels and would sell their mothers for one kobo if it advanced their petty and selfish causes."

As he said, this, I could feel the gentle whirl of the Blackberry in my pocket as it continued to capture the encounter.

The Speaker took a look at his wristwatch and winced. "It is already three o'clock and I still need to see a few more Members," he said as he quickly finished his drink and got up.

As I saw him to the door, I kept wondering how he was going to end this interview.

At the door, he suddenly turned round. "Hon. Samuel, you and I are from the North. In addition we are both lawyers, so we need to respect our *esprit de corps*, as they say in the military. You and I know why Wenike and his group want to get me out of my seat. It's just the first step in the long-term plan to install a Speaker who is the President's lackey. It is not about improving democracy in any way. It is all for a personal agenda which will soon gradually unfold. Let me urge you to back out from the group and join me in moving this democracy forward. As I said earlier on, there are several altruistic projects we can carry out within this National Assembly that will both improve the quality of governance in this country and, at the same time, benefit us individually as politicians. Wenike and his people are only being shortsighted. By the time I finish mapping out the programmes I have on my mind, they will look like fools."

As he said this, he brought out a brown envelope from his trouser pocket and held it out to me. "I know I cannot match the Presidency naira for naira but kindly take this small token for your urgent needs."

I quickly flinched away from his outstretched hand. "No sir, it is not necessary – I – I mean its, it's …"

"Oh come on Samuel, I know its nothing compared with the 10,000 dollars first instalment you got from Wenike before the start of your project as well as the 8,000 dollars you each received yesterday from the Presidency; but as I said earlier on, what we shall gain at the end of our own plans will be far greater than what you are currently witnessing with Wenike and his group.

I was dumbfounded. "How … how did you know?"

"Know what?"

"About the money I received and what we shared in my group."

In the stillness of the dawn, the Speaker's laughter echoed like an orchestra. "Samuel, I am not a novice in politics. As you have people spying on us, so we also have those spying on you. By the way, tell Wenike to tell the President that those boys who came to bug my office did a very bad job. Their footprints and handprints were all over the place. It didn't take my boys ten minutes to rig out all the so called sophisticated gadgets they planted in my office."

He brought out a small black gadget, the size of an average cellphone from his pocket.

"As for the Blackberry in your shirt pocket, Honourable Samuel, my Sony jamming device has neutralised its recording ability. It was a bold attempt by you to capture this discussion but, as I said, just join my group and I will take you to heights you never dreamt of reaching."

I was still staring at him in confusion and awe, the brown envelope lamely in my hand as the BMW sped away into the approaching dawn.

## CHAPTER

# 6

Long after the Speaker had left my house, I lay tossing and turning till the greying morning. My neighbour's dogs would not let me be as they held their concert in the middle of the street, barking and yelping to my distress. And as I thought over my short discussion with the Speaker, my mind was in turmoil.

"I cannot but shudder at the quality of the people you are associating with in your group."

As the Speaker's words came back to me, I started thinking deeply of my burden as a Honourable Member of the House of Representatives. Yes, the Speaker was right. Of all the Members in the Wenike group, I was about the best educated. Who of our group knew about Clausewitz? Or Plato? Or Socrates? Education and political gangsterism do not go well together. And instead of my current alignment with political gangsterism, I should use my education and experience as a lawyer in a more positive way: promoting bills and policies which would move the nation forward.

At least, that was what I told my father many years ago when I told him I wanted to become a lawyer. I made up my mind on my career the day Fulani herdsmen ransacked my village. I was about twelve then and my father and I had just finished harvesting the millet we grew that year. It was a good harvest, with the late millet still flowering on the farm in preparation for another full bloom.

It was our first good harvest after two difficult seasons when we had got nothing from the farm. We were all looking forward to the bumper harvest with the hope of making up for the loss of previous years. Then, the Fulani herdsmen and their cattle came! In one fell swoop, the cattle devoured all the millet stacked ready for the market. The crops on the farm were also not spared as the animals uprooted and chewed the green plants.

My father, weak and weary from tilling the land in difficult times, tried to fight back together with my other brother and me, but the Fulanis were too powerful for us. They beat us with their *sondas* and wounded my brother, almost severing his left earlobe with their sharp daggers.

We ran to the nearest police station to make a report but before we got back to the village with policemen, the Fulanis had disappeared. They were like spirits, appearing now with their cattle and disappearing the next moment.

What followed after this were harrowing days when my father had to sell off some of his farm implements to pay his debts. These were debts which he had hoped to pay with the millet harvest and send my brother and me to school with whatever remained.

I can still recollect my mother crying hours on end, lamenting the loss that would prevent her sons from attending school. It was her tears that made me decide to become a lawyer. On that memorable day, I told my father that I didn't want to become a farmer like him … "*Ni bana son in zama manomi,*" I told him in Hausa.

He was sitting outside at the veranda of our mud hut with his eyes tightly closed as if fighting vehemently against the recall of an unpleasant sight. His face was gaunt, dry and harsh, cruelly bitten by the merciless sun. I sat close to his left leg and whispered my resolve to him. He sat there motionless, seemingly oblivious of my presence. I repeated my resolve, this time louder.

No response again. I was not sure if he had heard me or not.

Perhaps he had but was only pretending not to. He was a hardworking and honest man who had made a success of the farming career he inherited from his father. So it was a family tradition which deep inside him, he would love to pass on to his sons. He had to leave me out of this.

I stood up straight in his front and shouted, *Ni lauya kawai nake son in zan zama* ... I want to become a lawyer!"

His closed eyes snapped open. "Did I hear you well, my son?"

"I want to be a lawyer."

Suddenly, my father's countenance brightened; for a brief moment, he seemed to be searching through his memory for his own inadequate schooling days and wondering if he too should have gone to school instead of tilling the land. I watched him transform before my very eyes. He was impressed, no doubt. Until now all that mattered to him were his corn, millet and the farm implements. But now something unexpected was happening.

He fixed his greyish-brown eyes on me, and asked, "You say you want to be a lawyer. Why?"

"Because I want to deal with those Fulanis who are always destroying our crops."

He looked at me with more admiration. "but I don't have any money to send you to school," he said.

"Don't worry, Baba, God will provide. I will fell trees and do manual labour. I just want to be a lawyer. I want to fight for the rights of farmers. It is high time this oppression stopped."

I realised that I had set an agenda for myself, a difficult agenda which became my passion for the next few years. I was going to be a lawyer. I was going to spend the rest of my life defending the oppressed, the poor and the weak. It sounded like a childish pledge but that was what I was determined to do.

I do not know exactly what our discussion that evening did to my father's psyche but I know that since then we became closer than we were before. To further strengthen this love, I won an Interior Missionary Scholarship which saw me through the University and Law school. It was like the icing on the cake. My parents almost worshipped me.

However, throughout my ten years of legal practice, save for one or two cases, I never once considered fulfilling my childhood desire to fight the Fulanis. All I was interested in was how to make money and ascend the social ladder.

Even after becoming a lawyer, the lure, the furious passion for money and position, had erased my original motive for studying law. The death of my beloved father did not help matters either. It was as if all the agitation against the menacing destruction of farm crops by the Fulani herdsmen was interred with him. I faced life as it presented itself.

Now, as the Honourable Speaker exited, my eyes began to open. "There are several altruisic things we can do together in this parliament. There are important bills and projects that we can consider," his voice kept reverberating. The more I thought of the Speaker's word, the more emboldened I got at what lay ahead for me. That was the moment when I determined my future in the parliament. I was still smiling at my self-discovery, when the muezzin at the nearby mosque called the early morning prayers.

"*Lafiya kika tashe ni da sassafe!?* Why are you getting me out of bed so early in the morning?" Elizabeth cursed as she finally opened the door after I had pressed her door bell several times.

"I'm sorry Lizzy, it is an emergency. The Speaker was in my house early this morning."

"The Speaker in your house?" Lizzy asked, looking stunned as if something had just hit her on the head.

Despite her dishevelled appearance in her nightgown, I could not but notice how alluring she was. Her disorganised hair and tired-looking eyes both added to her sex appeal.

She slowly led me back into her flat where she sat on a

settee, a small pillow discreetly placed between her thighs. She gave me one of those hard looks that has made her an important figure in the political calculation of Kaduna state and the National Assembly.

"Yes, you said that the Speaker was in your house? Lizzy asked, crossing her beautiful legs.

"Yes" I replied, watching the line of her long legs and enjoying the tension that was building up in the room. When I noticed that she was still staring at me with those lovely but hard eyes of hers, I quickly recounted what had happened with the Speaker.

Lizzy did not reveal any emotion as she listened to my story. It was when I told her my decision that she flew into a rage. "Samuel, you are not serious, you can't change your mind. Its too late to back out of the project, particularly after you had collected that hefty amount of money."

"I will return the money," I said.

"*Wasa kake Samuel, ka san za ka iya rasa ranka* ... you are joking Samuel, you can be killed."

"I don't mind dying for my conviction, especially having realised that I have been misled all along."

Lizzy recrossed her legs. I glanced down to where she was now rubbling her slender ankles. I was still staring when she repeated her question.

"Who misled you?"

"I ... I was misinformed about what it takes to effect an impeachment. You see, Lizzy, impeaching the Speaker is not an easy affair. We need two-thirds of the members to do this – not just of those present on the floor, but two-thirds of 360 members."

"Give me another excuse," Lizzy said.

"Moreover, I don't think that the reason we have for impeaching the Speaker is strong enough; we can use the threat of impeachment to get some favours from him but not an absolute impeachment."

Elizabeth continued staring at me for a moment without saying a word.

"Any more stupid excuses?" she finally said after a long pause.

It was now my turn to stare back at her.

After a few awkward minutes, the yellow wall clock chimed six o clock, and Lizzy spoke.

"Samuel, I thought you were a reasonable and reliable fellow. At least, that was what I said to Hon. Wenike when I told him about you. Not only did I vouch for your integrity, I promised him that you were like a brother to me. That was why you were made one of the members of the inner group with complete access to our secrets. You now want to back out after all I have gone through on your behalf? If you had told me that you needed more money, I would have given it to you. But for you to collect money from the Speaker, only to turn round and give me stupid excuses, is indefensible. Now, tell me, Samuel, how much the Speaker gave you, and I will double it."

"It's, it's – not about money, Lizzy," I said with difficulty. "Its about conviction. The Speaker just made me realise that I could do more for the parliament by bringing up quality bills and motions instead of this threat of impeachment."

"Samuel, you have not answered my question. *Nawa ya ba ka?* How much did the Speaker give you?" Lizzy repeated, fixing me with those sexy eyes of hers.

At that moment, however, I refused to be intimidated. I got up and told her I was not going to answer her question. And as I made for the door, she asked, "Where are you going?"

"To the Speaker, of course," I told her with a new found determination. "We have a press conference in his office later today."

Lizzy rose quickly to her feet, and came so close to me that I could smell her breath, faintly alcoholic from the previous night's revelry.

"I warn you, Samuel, Hon. Wenike is dangerous, he won't

allow you to leave the group; not after all the money and secrets you've had access to."

"I have told you that I will return his money. I have not spent it.

"How about all the information in your possession? He won't allow you to go; rather, he will … er … er."

"Go on, Lizzy, why are you hesitating, you mean to say that he will kill me? You think I am dumb enough not to know what Wenike can do?'

I moved close to her and stabbed my forefinger at her. "Look here, I am not afraid of anybody, not even Wenike or that bloody hooligan Kasali. I have a right to do what I want and nobody, I repeat nobody, can stop me. *Ja da baya ga rago ba tsoro bane* … it is not for cowardice that a ram retreats during a fight. Let them try me and see."

Apparently flustered by my audacity, Lizzy suddenly burst into tears. She fell into my arms as the pain and worry of the past few days finally took their toll. Her body shook convulsively as she sobbed until there seemed no more tears left. That was when I recovered from the shock of seeing her cry. I had never known that Lizzy whom I had seen as fearless and combative could ever cry. I always thought that she was in perfect control of things.

"I am sorry, Lizzy, I never knew you would react this way; but I can't go on with the impeachment plan. I don't see any good in it. I have discovered a better way to make my own contribution to this democracy."

Lizzy was quiet for a while. Then slowly she drew away from me and used the sleeve of her nightgown to wipe her face.

"Samuel, you can't back out now. I have promised Wenike that you are my brother and that he can trust you; please, don't do this to me. Apart from our sponsors who might be offended and demand a refund of their money, we shall lose face in the house, not to talk of the imminent danger we all face. Please, Samuel, I am ready to co-operate with you," she said hesitatingly.

"Co-operate with me over what?" I asked, admiring her hair which, despite the disorder, still glowed in the yellow lights of the chandelier.

"Over your former request," she said as she approached me again. Giggling, she unbuttoned the top of her nightgown to reveal two perfectly formed breasts. Smiling wickedly, she lifted her left breast towards me. "Come, Samuel, you have always wanted this."

I was still staring at the dark rigid nipple when the doorbell rang.

# CHAPTER

# 7

It was raining as I drove out of the Legislators' Quarters in Apo later in the day. That was after the doorbell had saved me from Lizzy's temptingly tantalising embonpoint. I had thought only boxers in trouble or torture were saved by the bell! Now I knew better. It was amazing that after more than a year of laying siege to Lizzy's charms, I could not convert the opportunity when it fell on my laps. Well, my consolation was that the opportunity was not a golden one. Rather, it was a Greek gift, a tainted one for that matter. No biting the bait! In the straight contest between desire and decision, between lust and conviction, I had won. A real pity, because, even though I loved her so much, I would not be blindfolded to reality on a courtesan's lap to stay in a project that I no longer believed in.

Now, as I approached the main gate of the Legislators' Quarters, I could make out the several screaming newspaper headlines as vendors jostled for the attention of motorists.

*I AM LIKE AN IROKO TREE – SPEAKER YAYA; SPEAKER'S REMOVAL FINAL; PRESIDENT BEHIND SPEAKERS'S WOES; NEW SPEAKER EMERGES TOMORROW; MACE TRACED TO PRESIDENTIAL VILLA!*

Almost all the newspapers headlines flashed the news of the crisis at the House of Representatives. And while the pro-government papers such as the *Daily Messenger* and the *Nigerian*

*Mail* were positive that the Speaker would survive the crisis, the opposition papers such as the *Telegraph* and the *Abuja Echo* had already confirmed his exit from office. Other newspapers even mentioned some mouth-watering amount of money as having exchanged hands as bribes. I went through a few, picking up both government and opposition papers.

I found the Speaker and his principal officers already waiting in the Speaker's office at the White House. Judging from their red eyes and husky voices, they must have passed another sleepless night. The Speaker had told them about me, for they all greeted me warmly.

"Deputy Speaker, are we ready?" the Speaker asked about ten minutes later.

"Almost sir, we are still waiting for more members, especially Hon. Muktar and Hon. Okoro."

With the arrival of Muktar and Okoro a few minutes later, we moved to Hearing Room One, the venue of the press conference. The place was jam-packed with journalists from both the print and electronic media, all eager to get a scoop of the day's great news.

Muktar, who had also defected from the Wenike group, was glad to see me. He quickly sat next to me and gave me a warm handshake. After we had been told to turn off our mobile phones, the Speaker started the press conference.

"Gentlemen of the press, I want to thank you all for coming to this very important conference," he began. "I want to specially thank our colleagues who have just joined us from the other group. It is heartening to know that they have finally seen through the deceit of the Wenike group. Honestly, I don't know what anybody will gain from causing disaffection and confusion among people. It is obvious that the reasons given for the impeachment are spurious and cannot hold. It is seven days today since the inglorious incident of the missing mace took place. Since then, we have done all that is humanly possible to make peace with everybody. While I am happy that some of our colleagues have decided to embrace peace, others have remained adamant. I had adjourned the sitting of the house by a week but now it is obvious that a week will not be enough. I am therefore adding another week to the adjournment. It is my hope that before this week ends things will have returned to normal."

As the Speaker read from a prepared speech, more Members joined the meeting. I looked round. It was obvious that the Speaker's late night visits had been very productive. I could count no fewer than ten Members who were formerly with the Wenike group. As the television cameras zoomed in on us, I knew that the press conference would cause a lot of stir in the Wenike group and by extension the Presidency.

Ten minutes later, when the Speaker finished his speech, the journalists descended on him with questions.

"Hon. Speaker, we understand that the mace is with the President."

"Is it true that the Wenike group has already secured a two-thirds majority for your impeachment?"

"Don't you think it is dangerous for you to continue to adjourn the sitting of the House when the mace is with your opponents?"

"Is it true that you have spent about one million dollars in order to get some Members of the Wenike group on your side?"

The questions were many, but the Speaker was able to adequately answer them all. He concluded by saying that every effort would be made to woo more Members away from the impeachment plan. He also promised not to discipline any Member of the opposition.

Despite the Speaker's efforts, more journalists continued to ask questions. I decided to flip through some newspapers to while away the time. Suddenly, a news item in the *Abuja Echo* caught my attention; FARMERS AND HERDSMEN CLASH IN KADUNA. I quickly read the story.

"A group of Fulani herdsmen last week encroached on farmlands in Kachia, Kaduna State, and destroyed crops that were ready for harvest. Even crops that were already harvested and awaiting removal from the farms were not spared by the rampaging livestock." The picture of my late father fighting frantically to rescue his crops flashed through my mind. I closed my eyes to shut the image off. I opened them again and continued to read.

"When the farmers discovered that their produce was being eaten by the livestock, mostly sheep and rams, often referred to as *Udah*, they reacted and the herdsmen started shooting them with arrows. As a result, some of the farmers sustained serious injuries. They were rescued and taken to the Kachia General Hospital for medical treatment."

As I read the piece, I felt my blood rise as unpleasant memories of my childhood came back to me. The news item was a replica of what my father had gone through more than thirty years earlier. Obviously, nothing had changed. The perennial clashes between farmers and herdsmen, an issue that I had promised my late father to help redress, were sadly still happening. It was the same issue that had motivated me to study law in the first instance.

Now that I was on the Speaker's side and with his promise to engage me in the pursuit of "altruistic" democratic activities in the house, I decided there and then that once the crisis of the impeachment was over, I would personally bring in a Bill that would once and for all stop these clashes between the farmers and the herdsmen.

As we later escorted the Speaker back to his office, I told him of my plans. He was delighted at my proposal.

"That is exactly the kind of thing I meant when I told you of some altruisic things we can do for this parliament. As a Fulani myself, I am eager that we put these sordid incidents behind us. You can therefore be assured of my co-operation in bringing in a good Bill that will once and for all put a stop to these nefarious activities … *je ka fara aiki akan bill din* … go and start work immediately on the Bill, my brother."

I was elated by the Speaker's views on my proposed project. That he could even be that accomodating in spite of what he was going through was very remarkable. This gesture more than ever increased my admiration of the honourable gentleman.

As expected, the Speaker's press conference caused not so much a stir as an earthquake in many quarters.

Senator Kayode Smollet was in his office in the basement of the White House when the Nigeria Television Authority (NTA) aired the first edition of the press conference at three in the afternoon. And as the middle-aged former serving Senator and now Presidential Liaison Officer at the National Assembly saw the number and quality of Honourable Members with the Speaker at the press conference, he broke out in a cold sweat. Despite the air conditioned room, he felt a burning heat in his body. He knew he had to act fast if he wanted to avoid the President's wrath.

Quickly, he reached for his mobile phone and called Hon. Linus Wenike who was at that time oblivious of what was happening, having just woken up. So worried was Senator Smollet that he did not wait for Wenike to come and see him in his office as he had promised. Rather, Smollet quickly drove to his house at the Apo Legislators' Quarters. When he arrived at Wenike's apartment at the zone B section of the quarters, he found the burly Member already at a meeting with some of his colleagues.

"Honourable, the President will be very upset at this development," Smollet said breathlessly on arrival at Wenike's sitting room. "I thought that by now, the Speaker's camp would have emptied and then we could move in with our killer plan. Unfortunately, the fellow has captured even more of our members especially some key ones."

"Try to relax, Senator," Wenike said as he sipped from a glass of brandy in his hand. "We have not lost any key Member."

"But – but – Honourable, I saw Hon. Muktar and Hon. Bakura among others with the Speaker."

"Heh heh, so what? Is it Bakura and Muktar you are calling key Members?" Wenike snorted. "Those are small boys. Their absence can't deter us. You just wait. By the time I put my next plan into action, many of them will be begging to be back in our group."

"In addition," Hon. Elizabeth said, "some of them are actually in the Speaker's group on our behalf. They are not really with the Speaker. Its part of our master plan."

"Em … em … Hon. Lizzy, are you sure? The way I saw those Members, they seemed very committed to the Speaker's group."

Wenike went to the side cabinet to refill his glass. "Senator, please relax. This is politics, it is not over until it is over. You just see what will happen. The Speaker thinks he is wise by adjourning the sitting of the house by another week. He thinks he can use that to fend off his impeachment. He is joking. Tomorrow, we shall convene a parallel sitting of the house where his impeachment will be a fait accompli.

"But … but … Honourable, how do you want to do that? Do you have enough Members to effect the impeachment?"

Suddenly Wenike burst out laughing. "Senator, with due respect, I thought you were a politician? This is not the first impeachment exercise I have organised. Apart from the one we carried out during the last legislative session, my services have also been contracted by no fewer than five State Houses of Assembly that I have helped to impeach their Speakers. You therefore have nothing to fear. I don't want to give you the details of what we shall do tomorrow. Rest assured, though, that the authentic House of Representatives session will sit tomorrow at a venue that I will let you know later tonight. All we need from you is some money with which to fine-tune the logistics."

Despite Wenike's assurances, Senator Smollet was still not convinced.

"Before I can get more money, the President will want to know the details. You know how stingy that bloody fellow is. I can't just go to him and ask for more money. I need to convince him what the money is for and without the details, he may not answer me."

Wenike was now getting restless and angry as the high-grade alcohol he had been consuming since afternoon started taking effect. He glared in the direction of the Senator. "I cannot give you any more details than I have done for security reasons. If the President is no more interested in the plan he should let us know; then we can all go home and rest. We have spent countless sleepless nights and quantities of money, not to talk of the attendant risk, and all you talk about is what to tell one bloody President who doesn't know his right hand from his left. Does he think impeaching a Speaker of the Federal House of Representatives is an easy thing? Or does he want to compare this with impeaching Speakers of ordinary State Houses of Assembly? Senator, in order to reassure your master the President, our methodology is this and I hope you will keep it away from the press."

'Ha ha, of course Honourable, I will, ' the Senator said.

"All right, then. This is it. Tomorrow morning, we shall go to the Nicon Hilton conference room with the mace and elect a Speaker pro tempore. After this, we shall suspend all the Members in the former Speaker's group. That leaves us with the Members of our own group. From there, we shall get two-thirds of our group to impeach the former Speaker. Once that is done, we write to Mr. President to open the parliament for us and we move in with our own Speaker. All the suspended Members are then given two weeks to apologise or face further sanctions. That's all; you will see how those Members who left our group will be begging to come back."

As he finished, the shouts of "Leader! Leader! Leader!" rent the small flat as more Members of the group arrived and started jubilating at what they considered a master stroke. Delighted with the way things had turned out, Senator Smollet quickly dashed to his car for the short drive to the Presidential villa.

# CHAPTER 8

"You must be out of your mind to expect me to believe all this junk. This kindergarten drivel ..." This was the President and Commander-in-Chief of the Nigerian Armed Forces, Chief Ambrose Oneya, expressing his rage after being briefed by Senator Smollet on the latest developments in the House of Representatives. "Honourable Members, or a rag-tag team of miscreants? Only a pea-brained idiot will embark on such a stupid, nonsensical, illiterate, ill-advised and unintelligent adventure."

Senator Smollet broke out in cold sweat. "But Mr. President ..."

The President made a sweeping gesture with his hands. "Smollet, you disappoint me. You have very badly disappointed me. What did you read at university?"

"History, Mr. President."

"Little wonder you have a primitive mentality and a museum mind. Such idiocy! They want to go to the lobby of a hotel, suspend members of the Speaker's group and impeach the Speaker on the strength of the hare-brained notion that they are in possession of the bloody mace. Is that how impeachments are effected? Read your history, Smollet and give me one instance, just one instance, down the long calendar of centuries where such a fatuous plan was effected?"

The President paused. "Sit down, Smollet", he said.

Smollet sat down.

The President grimaced. He asked, "Senator Sunday Kayode Smollet, student of history… or is it graduate of History, you are my Liaison Officer?"

"Yes Sir," Smollet said.

"A grand title for a small man, I must say." The President started to shout. "How on earth could you, a former Senator of the Federal Republic of Nigeria, have swallowed all that rubbish into your small stomach and regurgitated same to me triumphantly only to announce to me, the son of my mother, Madam Veronica Virginia Oneya, that I should bring money for this madcap project. Will you remove your obnoxious presence from my sight and return in two minutes' time?"

Smollet vanished.

Mohammed Danladi, the Principal Secretary to the President, found himself in a fix. He was devoted to the President, yes; at the same time the Speaker was a distant relative of his. Naturally, the Speaker had his sympathy. On certain occasions in the past he had discreetly passed information to the Speaker. Now after the President's emotional outburst and peremptory dismissal of Senator Smollet, Mohammed knew he was expected to pour oil on troubled waters and soothe the President's nerves. He cleared his throat.

Smollet reappeared.

The President snapped. "It is not yet two minutes. There are ten seconds to go!"

The Senator vanished again, only to reappear in seconds, staring at the wall clock in anticipatory justification.

Mohammed turned to Smollet. "Senator Smollet, permit me to ask you one simple question. Are you sure that this group has the required two-thirds majority to impeach the Speaker? As my arithmetic goes, two-thirds of 360 is 240. Do you have two hundred and forty men ready, willing and able for this exercise? That is my question."

Smollet, his fury suppressed said, "Yes, they do. You see, that is the reason they want to suspend all the Members in the

Speaker's group so that …"

"So that what?" the President interrupted, "Do they have the power to suspend anybody… even a chef … in a hotel?"

"I … I think …" Smollet began.

"Think! After frittering-away two million dollars and making me, the very son of my mother, Madam Veronica Virginia Oneya, a laughing stock in the press! By the way, my friend where is the mace?"

"In my office, Sir."

"And you, Smollet, the son of *your* mother, whoever she is, gave grounds for the press to editorialise, cartoonise and satirise that the mace was with me, me, President of the Federal Republic of Nigeria; me, the very son of my honourable longsuffering mother Madam Veronica Virginia Oneya. The mace with you? You are '*Small*-let' indeed. I should smite you, Smollet."

"I am sorry, Your Excellency."

"You can't liaise properly with the legislature. You cannot manage the Press. And my Principal Secretary knows more about impeachment than you. If Yaya is not off in the next seven days, you are out. Out! you hear? out, out, out!"

Smollet said, "I handed …"

"You heard me," the President bellowed, "out with you!'

Smollet scrambled off.

"Mohammed, bring my special drink and tell small Smollet to come and complete his rotten report in the next five minutes."

\* \* \*

The 'special drink' had calmed the President.

Smollet came back in, "I handled them well. We got positive reports in *The Clarion, The Ambassador, The Clean Broom* and others. Only *The Outsider* and *The Radical* were out of line. They were the ones writing rubbish about you, claiming the mace was with you …"

"And you did not write an instant rebuttal, refutal and denial?"

"We did, Sir."

"So why did they continue to cry that I, the Honourable son of my honourable mother Madam Veronica Virginia Oneya, had the mace with me?"

"In the interest of sensational and eccentric journalism Sir!"

"Then you have to sue them. Liaise with the Attorney-General and prepare suits against them. Sue them, you hear, sue them! Also next month, I want every ministry, every parastatal, and every agency, federal, state and local, to book newspaper space for congratulatory messages to my mother on her birthday. With her full photogragh. A full page. No quarter-page nonsense, you hear?"

"Yes, Sir."

"She will be eighty-five but they must use her photograph when she was twenty-five. That was when my beautiful mother gave birth to me, the very, very, very beautiful Madam Veronica Virginia Oneya. Now, where was I?"

Smollet quickly recovered his wits. "We have to sue the press."

"Yes, sue the opposition press. No birthday adverts for my mother must appear in them. Now complete your rotten report in two minutes flat."

Smollet continued, "We are in control, your Excellency …"

"Which rotten control? Two million dollars down the drain and that Yeye Yaya went on the NTA speaking fine grammar at a press conference. In control! In control my big toenail. All the chaps have crossed carpet to Yeye Yaya. All that Wenike thug knows is money for logistics. Is that not so?"

"Yes, Your Excellency. But what you saw on TV is not the true picture of things. Not all those chaps belong to Yaya. They are our boys, our spies. Consider, Sir, we are on top of things. Consider our spies; consider that we have the mace. We hold the upper hand. The mace is the authority of the parliament. Nobody is above the mace."

"Where is that, Smollet, in the constitution?"

"It is not there, Sir …"

"When did you become a liar?"

"No, yes, I mean, it is not in the National Constitution but it is part of the rules and regulations binding the legislature …"

"Enough. That is what you should have said, Smollet."

Smollet continued to persuade the President until he was able to get him back on his side. It was only then that Chief Oneya was mollified and agreed to help but only on the condition that the Wenike group sit at the National Assembly Building and not at the hotel.

"That will be difficult …"

"Smollet, always think positively. Have you ever read Norman Vincent Peale's *The Power of Positive Thinking*? The moment it arrived in our school library in 1962, I was the first to read it."

"Yes, sir. Thinking positively, Sir, acting positively, Your Excellency we shall have to get round the problems created by Speaker Yaya. He locked up the chamber. Moreover, the access road to the place is always locked."

The President snorted. "That does not mean a thing to me. We have the Federal might. I will arrange for security men to escort the Wenike group to the place tomorrow so that they can sit."

"We shall need the keys to the chamber," Smollet suggested.

"Don't worry about that. Our men will make sure that the chamber doors are opened. Once the Wenike group can sit in the chamber of the House of Representatives with the mace, the sitting becomes legal. That is all."

"Em …em … not really, Your Excellency," Smollet began. "We still have to drop something …"

"I don't want to hear anything about money," the President said.

"But Sir, you cannot make an omelette without breaking eggs. We need the money."

"Yes, Mohammed," the President said.

"Sir, I think ..." Mohammed started.

The President smiled. "But why do we always have to give them something before a project, Mohammed? I thought this should come after, not before."

"Sir, I think they need some money as motiva-tion," Mohammed said.

The President scowled. Mohammed flinched. Smollet gazed at the ceiling.

"How much?"

Smollet rummaged in the folds of his *agbada* and brought out a pocket calculator. Smacking his lips in anticipation of what lay ahead of him, he pressed a few buttons. He showed the President the figure.

"What!! All that money after what we had already spent?" the President roared as if stung by a scorpion.

"We also have to sort out the journalists sir. That's the only way we can stop the hostile reports."

"Okay. Cut it by twenty per cent."

"Okay, your excellency." Smollet said.

Abruptly, the President held Smollet by his collar and posed the question, "Smollet, do you like my mother?"

"Yes, I do, Sir."

"Now, arrange a birthday gift for her. Every ministry, agency, parastatal, state, local government and the wards of the Total Party must drop 'something'. One million naira each ..."

"Yes, Sir,"

"That is that."

In his corner, Mohammed Danladi was already sending an urgent text message to his cousin, the Speaker.

\* \* \*

The text message from the Speaker was disturbing; "Drop everything and come to the office." It was all the more worrying because I had just left the office after a marathon meeting. I was so worried. I skipped lunch and drove straight to the White House. What could be the matter, I wondered. At the last meeting, positive signals had come that the President was making moves to reconcile the opposing groups, following the peace-making efforts of the party leadership.

At the office, I found huddled around the Speaker some Members and the whole leadership of the House. They were all pensive. The Speaker went straight to the point.

"We have information that Wenike and his group will be sitting in the chamber tomorrow."

"How do they intend to do that?" I asked.

"Our information again is that the President has promised to give them enough security. The lock of the chamber will be picked to allow the upstarts to have their despicable sitting."

Silence permeated the office as the enormity of what had been said sank in. We were all worried; clearly, with the security personnel behind them, Wenike and his group would have a smooth ride with their foul plot. I was the first to break the silence.

"Mr. Speaker, I doubt the authenticity of this information. It beats me how the President would allow the forcible removal from office of a democratically elected Speaker. It does not ring true. It just is not right."

The leader spoke. "That was also my first thought at the news. However, we have no cause to doubt the reality of our source."

"It's okay, Leader," the Deputy Speaker came in. "Debating whether the information is true or false is not the issue here and now. We have confirmed the information, gentlemen. The point is we must act and act fast! We have just a little less than twelve hours to put our countermeasures in motion." The Deputy Speaker paused to blow his nose into a handkerchief.

"We don't have the security force to counter the forces of government. Our best bet therefore is to resort to the use of mass action. I do not need to preach the power of mass action to you. It has worked in other countries. It worked in Cambodia; it worked in Tibet and it worked up to a point in Tiananmen Square in China. Only two things are necessary, gentlemen: proper organisation and utmost secrecy. Leave the organisation of the market men, drivers, artisans and other workers to me. Our Leader, a former School Principal and able teacher for many years, will reach out to teachers at all levels and civil servants of all cadres. Samuel is a former student leader and will mobilise the students; Honourable Fatimata will link us with the market women.

Fatimata sprang up as if stung by a bee. "Hold it there, Mr. Speaker," she snapped, removing her spectacles in the same movement. "Are you trying to say you want to line up innocent defenseless people against the might of tanks and guns?"

"Not exactly," the Deputy Speaker replied.

"Count Honourable Fatimata and the market women out of any suicidal confrontation, exact or inexact, with the might of tanks and guns. If there are no useful ideas here, I am going home."

"No, that is not what we are saying. Sit down, please, Honourable Fatimata, and hear me out. The Presidency is brimming with firepower and funds. Therefore our best bet is to seek out, develop and mobilise the might of the masses, of our people. The plan is for us to get as many people as possible into the National Assembly premises and form a human wall against the Wenike group. Of course, the journalists will be on hand to capture the event, which I am sure will attract the attention of the world press. Once we do this, the Wenike group will certainly see reason and withdraw. The worst scenario is a few days' stand-off before we succeed; but succeed we surely will."

"Just like the Tiananmen Square event," I added as the Deputy Speaker nodded before succumbing to another bout of sneezing.

Quiet reigned once again in the room. It dawned on everyone that the nation's soul was under serious threat and drastic action must be taken to protect it. More Members came in and the scraping of dragged chairs filled the room.

Honourable Moses Adeyi from Oyo State broke the silence. "Is it possible to look for another mode of confrontation? You heard Honourable Fatimata. How can we lead innocent people as lambs to the slaughter? How can we form a wall with defenceless citizens as cannon fodder? Soldiers are mad dogs and policemen are hungry puppies. All this fine talk about China and Tiananmen Square is neither here nor there. Ladies and gentlemen, China is not Nigeria and Nigeria is not China. Why am I even talking? Our people love their lives, *o jare*. You will be lucky to find people to agree to do what you want. Patriotism is alien to Nigerian soil. Who will stand up for anything except his stomach? All people want is money to eat."

Fatimata had listened intently all along, nodding at every point. She added. "How can you drag all these people into the premises of the National Assembly under the nose of the security forces? You are toying with arrests, tortures, court action… Good old Chief Oneya will throw in charges of treason for good measure."

The Leader raised his hands like a policeman signalling a car to stop. "How to sneak in under the nose of security forces is a strategic challenge that we have studied and met head on. We have that all worked out. Now will people come out? They will, my dear Fatimata. Gentlemen, they will. We shall get enough people for our cause. Leave the details of the operation to us. The one thing we must do is keep our mouths shut. No babbling to the press. No word to madam at home or to your husbands. Mum's the word. Your duty as a group is to agree to the plan. We, your leaders will ensure execution."

"But what about my suggestion? It is as if nobody wants to consider what I said," Honourable Moses Adeyi said.

"What did you say?" asked the Deputy Speaker.

"You see now, you weren't even listening, DS. What kind of ..."

"How did you know I wasn't listening? I was all ears, only my attention drifted," the Deputy Speaker said.

The Leader came in. "Adeyi's suggestion was that we should look for another way out of the crisis."

The Deputy Speaker's patience snapped. "Like what and what? Be specific. This is no time for fancy seminars or nitpicking academics. We have to be practical."

Honourable Adeyi's voice raised a pitch. "Dialogue, ladies and gentlemen, dialogue. Until we exhaust all avenues of dialogue we have not started on the right foot at all. Let us approach the party leaders to intervene. Let us approach the foreign diplomats. Let us talk to the press, local and international. We have to look ..."

"The clock is running too fast for that now, Hon. Moses," the Speaker interrupted. "Fortunately we have attempted all you have said. You are perhaps new to the group but I can tell you truthfully that we worked in small units to initiate dialogue. Nothing happened. Our efforts were ignored by the President. He has our party in a vice-like grip. You can't talk with the party leaders. They are all on his side."

"Including the party chairman?" Moses asked.

"Yes, including the chairman. You know what he said? He said, 'Yaya, resign or be impeached!' The foreign diplomats said, 'Start fighting first, later we shall join you and support your cause.' The press made the same promise, start the battle and we will come in full force on your side. It is not a bad situation. After all, they are all on our side. Our task is to mobilise people, enough people; bring the events to the attention of the press, local and international. Thus will the battle be won. All that is required of us is to start the process as soon as possible knowing fully well that Wenike and his group will strike tomorrow. Therefore we do not have any time to waste. We have to move now."

I rejoiced in my heart. The Speaker's words did the magic just as I expected. His words calmed all frayed nerves. We took a decision to go full speed on our plans. Those given specific assignments were formally briefed and funds allocated to their activities.

"The Deputy Speaker will oversee the details of our activities," the Speaker added. "We need to work very fast as all arrangements must be in place by four this afternoon. Our friends in the National Assembly Security Unit have told us that all the people we are bringing must be in the premises by midnight at the latest. As you are all aware, surprise is our greatest weapon. It is vital that the details of this operation be kept absolutely secret."

# CHAPTER

# 9

I spent most of that afternoon at the campus of the University of Abuja mobilising students for our project, which we had codenamed 'Operation *Kyarkeci*'. *Kyarkeci* is the Hausa word for 'wild dog'.

In spite of the fearsome name *Kyarkeci*, we were convinced that with our plans in proper shape, the exercise would not only be successful but would also be executed without the shedding of any blood whatsoever.

Before I got to the campus, Honourable Suleiman, Member representing the Federal Capital Territory, had utilised his political network to reach out to the students. This was not too difficult, as many of the students had assisted him earlier, in the course of his election campaign. At first the student union leaders raised their voices against what they called 'being dragged into the morass of partisan politics'. When we made them understand that our group had a pan-Nigerian membership cutting across ethnic, regional, religious and political divides, they decided to join us. Their ire was roused at the news that it was the President's long reach that was roiling the waters of the legislature. When they were told that the President had issued a command for members of the armed forces to operate against us, the students were further incensed.

Our plan was to get some five hundred students each from

the University of Abuja and Nasarawa State University. However, by the close of the first day, more than seven hundred students from the University of Abuja alone had given their consent as volunteers; what this meant was that we had to make arrangements for extra buses to convey all the students. The moment we finished our task in Abuja, we dashed across to Nassarawa State University, Keffi. Here again, the Honourable Member representing Nasarawa Federal constituency took it upon himself to mobilise the students. It was our luck that the students at the University of Abuja were in a slack period. They had finished their examinations and were fighting the ensuing boredom. We were not as lucky at Nasarawa State University. A young state university was not likely to have on its student roll the kind of adventurous souls to be found at the older Federal University of Abuja. Taking the utmost care to prevent information leakage, we were able to mobilise just three hundred students. It appeared that our biggest problem was with the market women. Many of them were under the leadership of the wife of the TDP chairman in the Federal Capital Territory. A highly intelligent lady and up-and-coming politician, Fatimata had quickly withdrawn from the women when she realised they were becoming suspicious of her efforts.

Our luck was better with the workers. The Deputy Speaker wisely bypassed the individual unions, going straight instead to the leadership of the Nigeria Labour Congress, who then used their own network to mobilise about two thousand workers. Honourable Salem suggested that we should dash to Kaduna and import *almajiris* for the exercise. The suggestion was turned down for two reasons: we were eager not to taint the exercise with any religious colouration, and we wanted to avoid the risk of moving such a crowd all the way from Kaduna to Abuja.

It was agreed that the workers would remain at the Nigeria Labour Congress headquarters in Wuse until a quarter to midnight, when they could be conveyed in Nigeria Labour Congress buses to the National Assembly. It was also agreed that students from the University of Abuja and Nasarawa State Assembly would remain on their campuses until eleven in the evening, when they would commence the approximately one-hour journey from their schools. We had succeeded in getting our friends in the National Assembly security unit to be on duty that evening. The plan was for them to open the back gate, usually closed at night. Once inside the National Assembly premises, we hoped to get the people waiting in the courtyard of the annexe building until six in the morning, when we were to move them to the security gates of the White House.

Foreign correspondents from the BBC, the VOA and CNN had been tipped off to be at the White House by six in the morning. Our own journalists had also been summoned. A few local television outfits whose transmitter stations had remained in the National Assembly premises since the beginning of the crisis had promised to start live recordings of the events as early as seven in the morning. I was summoned to a meeting in the Deputy Speaker's office at eight in the evening. Hungry and weary after spending the entire afternoon travelling between Gwagwalada and Keffi, I was glad to meet members tackling dinner when I reached the Deputy Speaker's office.

I joined the others in their rice and stew. The Deputy Speaker entered the office, a mobile phone glued to his right ear. He appeared restless. He was talking to some security personnel and he mentioned the need for them to have gas masks ready against tear gas. "There will surely be attempts to disperse the crowd with tear gas," he said. "Meanwhile, we have purchased some fifty litres of kerosene. Our people can soak their handkerchiefs in it and tie them across their noses against gas inhalation."

The Deputy Speaker finished speaking on the phone, and nodded to me to follow him into the inner office. Once inside, he walked briskly to the washbasin and scrubbed his hands. "Just a minute," he said, then brought out a small transparent sachet from the inner pocket of his gown. He took a pinch of powdery substance; closing first one nostril then the other, he inhaled the stuff and his already red eyes became watery in an instant. He shut his eyes for a moment to allow the drug to get into his brain. He grinned sheepishly and turned to me. "Want some?'

"No, thanks," I replied. "But what it is?"

He laughed. "So you don't know what it is and yet you said you don't want any?"

"I don't think I'd like anything that brought tears to my eyes and at the same time made my nose wet."

He looked surprised. "Sammy, Sammy, you mean you don't use anything?"

"Anything? You mean, things like …"

"Oh yes, cocaine, cannabis, good old alcohol …"

"No, no, no."

"Not even *gagaye*?"

"What's that?"

He burst out laughing, "*Burantashi*."

"No, no, no, I don't need such things. No stimulant whatsoever. A sex stimulant? Chai, my girlfriend has assured me that I am as strong as a horse. Unless I want to kill her, I cannot use any external aid."

"Sammy, Sammy, clean Sammy. The last moral man standing. Haba, a man is allowed one weakness, one indulgence. No, no, a politician must use something." He took another pinch of white powder. Then the penny dropped with me.

"I don't think you should be using that. Cocaine is no use. I have read a lot about it. When you take it you get an instant high that makes your brain believe you can do a day's job in an hour. The sad thing is that it can hurt your nostrils, really damage them. Cocaine is addictive and ultra-expensive: It has destroyed careers, reputations, important people. Quit, please."

The Deputy Speaker smiled. "Thanks for the little lecture. The task ahead of us is enormous. We all need a little 'something'. With this very big project on our hands I wanted to be kind to you and give you little push. Well, the reason I actually called you is to give you money for the operation."

He brought out a small Ghana-Must-Go bag, opened it and brought out a stack of currency notes.

"This heap is for the students. That one is for hiring buses. The third heap is for petrol."

"DS, what about refreshment?"

"Refreshments? Why?"

"Well, how can we keep students and workers from midnight until six in the morning without feeding them? In any case, who knows how long the standoff will last? We must stock food and drinks. We won't find food for three thousand people without adequate planning."

He fell silent, thinking. "Sammy, thank you, we did not factor feeding into the funds. I had imagined the students would take care of themselves from what we shall give them. Now that you have mentioned it, I will look into it.

\* \* \*

Senator Smollet had worked all day in his tiny office at the basement of the White House. Very early in the morning, he had accompanied the security team sent from the villa to the National Assembly where the lock of the chamber was picked and the cleaners sent in to clean up the place. The communication gadgets including the microphones were tested and found in good condition. All this while, two members of the Wenike group were busy in an adjoining office preparing the order papers as well as the motion for the impeachment of the Speaker.

At about three in the afternoon, Hons. Wenike, Kasali and Elizabeth gathered in Smollet's office for a brief meeting. Elizabeth asked, "Well, do we have any news or information from the Speaker's group?"

Wenike replied, "No news yet. Hon. Amunike has not reported anything. He is our man there. He only reported that the group has not met in the last four days."

"I don't trust Amunike's information," said Elizabeth. "When I was with them we used to meet every day. You know it was that pest Samuel that exposed me. Pestering, pestering, always pestering me. 'I like your dress. Your skin is fine. Let us go for dinner.' I never gave the randy goat a chance. What was I saying? *Ah, ah,* we used to meet every day. My feeling is that suspicion has fallen on Amunike and he has been sidelined, kept away from meetings, consultations, important decisions, and the whole ball game. You can't trust that randy pest who calls himself Samuel. He must have supplied them a complete list."

"You see what I was saying now," Wenike said. "I should have dealt with the so-and-so ages ago. He should be in the hospital or a mortuary by now. That saboteur! I never trusted him. I don't trust men who don't take anything. No drinks. No drugs. No cigarettes … not even women …"

"He wanted to take me now," Lizzy cut in. "The randy pest. May AIDS catch him or may he catch AIDS."

Wenike said. "Anyway, let him be. If we hit him the police will be hot on my heels. Let him be. They have failed anyhow. He is not that influential. He has little stomach for real politics."

"Enough of personalities," Smollet interjected. "Something tells me the Speaker and his group are up to something. They must know we have planned their funeral for tomorrow."

"What can they do, even if they know?" Wenike said. "We have mastered them. We have the backing of the government and they know it. In fact, left to me it will be better to send them an invitation card to tomorrow's event. The time for secrecy is over. Send them an invitation, I say. They will give up the moment they know being adamant will not pay them …"

Senator Smollet's phone rang all of a sudden and he motioned to Wenike to stop talking. "Yes, Your Excellency, all is set. No, I have not seen him… maybe … OK, Your Excellency. We shall do that, Sir. Thank you, Sir, OK, Your Excellency."

Smollet put away his phone and laughed uproariously. "You know what the President said? Security reports have told him students may demonstrate tomorrow in the Federal Capital Territory. The mobile policemen will take care of that. They have been drafted to take over the major roads tomorrow."

Wenike also laughed. "So that is all Yaya can do! His children's classmates are now his political foot soldiers. Hey, you there, bring out the champagne!"

"I told you," Senator Smollet said smugly, "I told you, the Speaker and his group have not been idle, only silent. They went underground to plan. Their plan is DOA, *ha! ha! ha!*"

Lizzy asked," What is DOA?"

"Dead on arrival," Wenike said, popping open the champagne bottle that an aide had brought. "Dead on arrival, I say," he continued. "Before the poor undergraduates clear their throats to sing solidarity songs, Yaya's political obituary will be out on the airwaves. The afternoon papers will sell out tomorrow."

"What will the students be demonstrating against?" Lizzy asked. Senator Smollet grinned. "What else? It is sure to be about the planned impeachment."

Kasali, who had been quietly nursing a bottle of Gulder, stabbed the air with his muscular arms. "What will an ordinary demonstration in the town do for them? Let them demonstrate. While they are busy singing, we will be busy impeaching."

"Give me champagne, *bo*," Elizabeth said amidst general laughter. "Now," said Senator Smollet, pulling out a Ghana-Must-Go bag from under a table, "my distinguished Honourables, back to business. Everything is here. It is up to us to sort things out."

Wenike, a glass of champagne in hand, looked up quizzically. "Everything?"

"I mean the logistics for the Members, security men and journalists and of course, my own fertilizer."

"No!" Wenike said. "You can't do that, Senator Smollet, you and I know the protocol of distribution. What we normally do is for you to handle the money for the security men and journalists and hand over our own to us in a lump sum."

"Well, you see. *Em*… I thought in view of the urgency of the situation that we should move fast, do it all together. You know. OK, we will follow the usual protocol." Smollet moved on. "Next is the arrangement for the plenary sitting. Wenike, how are you going to report, individually or will you rather come as a group?"

Members fell briefly silent, pondering the issue. Normal parliamentary procedure was clear: Members proceeded individually to the chamber. However, in view of the special situation, Members were rather doubtful about what to do. Going individually had its merits but congregating in a place and moving *en masse* to the National Assembly appeared to be a stronger option. The little debate see-sawed for a few minutes until it was resolved that the Members should congregate in front of Wenike's house, from where security men would lead them to the premises of the National Assembly in a convoy.

"We have forgotten the most important thing," Lizzy said.

Kasali coughed. "No, we have discussed fertilizer. There is no problem. Give me some champagne, now, Wenike."

Lizzy shook her head. "Honourable Tough-man Kasali, the strongman of Ibadan, terror of the Southwest, money is your own headache-oh! But I was thinking of the mace. Where is it? Who will bring it?"

Senator Smollet: "Thank you, Honourable Elizabeth. I have the mace with me. First thing tomorrow the Sergeant-at-Arms will come for it and take it to the office of the Speaker *pro tempore*, who will be led to the chambers at the right time."

"But, Senator," Kasali came in again, his eyes beginning to glint from the effects of the alcohol. "We have to guard the mace-oh. It must not be hijacked on the way-oh. You know, some of our colleagues may still be lurking around."

The Senator smiled," Kasali, I understand your fears. There is no problem. Security will be ultra-tight tomorrow."

# CHAPTER

# 10

Shortly before midnight, the last busload of students and workers entered the premises of the National Assembly. It had started to rain at about ten o'clock that night, a steady shower that was not heavy enough to disrupt the traffic or drive policemen away from their checkpoints. This, coupled with our decision to use different routes to the National Assembly, assisted in reducing suspicion. All went well except for an altercation between a driver of one of the Nigeria Labour Congress buses and two drunken security men. We were able to handle the situation before it got out of hand. This was due to a sudden change in the security details assigned to the back entrance. Our men had already made contacts with the first set of security men but the sudden change disorganised our plans and so we had to switch to the front entrance.

Earlier in the day, our contacts in the State Security Service had disseminated a false security report, alleging that the students of higher institutions were planning to stage a protest in the Federal Capital Territory business district. This canard was part of our effort to confuse the Presidency, created as a cover-up for what was sure to be noticed as an unusual mass movement of students and workers in buses.

As expected, the Presidency had reacted to the report by ordering more security forces to the city centre. This we expected to reduce the number of security forces in the National Assembly premises. To move in the crowd, we had about sixty buses, each seating fifty people. As soon as they had settled down in the open quadrangle of the annex building, where some canopies had been erected, the students and workers were served refreshments. Then the Deputy Speaker addressed the crowd. He was tired and dishevelled, but he had a glitter in his eyes still. I remembered his words, "You have to use something," and I smiled. His speech was powerful, a cocaine-fuelled performance. He thanked the people for their patriotism and courage. He then traced the genesis of the crisis in the House of Representatives to the greed and inordinate ambition of a few members who had held the majority hostage. The audience applauded rather noisily.

The Deputy Speaker raised his right hand in restraint. "Please, we cannot afford to draw attention to ourselves and our plans at this time. Let us listen in silence. Whereas other democracies such as our neighbour Ghana are making substantial progress in the governance of their people, what we are witnessing in our own parliament is of great concern to all. We call ourselves the giant of Africa but what we are doing to ourselves in the name of democracy is, to say the least, degrading. The tragedy of it all is that our President, who is supposed to be an impartial umpire in the whole situation, has chosen to take sides." The Deputy Speaker coughed slightly and continued. "This is in pursuit of his own selfish interests. The whole nation is witness to the laudable manner in which our parliament ensured that the current Speaker was elected without any interference or influence from the Presidency. This singular act, the very first in our democratic experience, proved a bitter pill for the President to swallow. Speculations, rumors and privileged opinion suggest that the President wants to replace the current Speaker with his own man as a prelude to an extension of his tenure in office beyond the constitutional two terms. The President has succeeded in his nefarious plan thus far because of the greed of some of our colleagues on the other side. The President has personally taken over the attempt to sack the Speaker illegally. It is also a matter of record that the house has been unable to conduct any reasonable business in the past two weeks. Apart from organising the illegal removal of the mace from the chamber, the President has now decided to provide security cover for a renegade section of the legislators to convene an illegal sitting tomorrow in the legislative chamber. Reports reaching us indicate that the group intends to force its way into the National Assembly with tanks and guns to sack Members not in their faction and to impeach the Speaker. This is where you come in. You are young men of honour and promise, torchbearers of democracy and good governance in the quest for a greater Nigeria. You are now the only people who can save the country from an ignominious descent into chaos and instability. You alone can lead the country in the march to the promised land of peace and prosperity. The whole country is looking up to you. Gathered here in Abuja, are foreign correspondents of major international news organisations such as the BBC, CNN, the VOA and Al Jazeera. You will, as from tomorrow, become the symbol of Democracy. You will have the eyes of the world focused upon you. You cannot afford to fail. And you will not fail. Let me remind you of the ennobling words of that great statesman, soldier, politician, writer and historian Winston Churchill, who said, 'To each comes in his or her lifetime a special moment when they are tapped on the shoulder and offered to do a very special thing, unique to them and fitted to their talent. What a tragedy if that moment finds them unprepared or unqualified for that which could have been their finest hour.' Ladies and gentlemen, your finest hour has come. You dare not fail. The whole world is watching and Nigeria is waiting ... God bless you all."

    Thunderous applause erupted from the crowd.

    "Good show, sir," I said, embracing the Deputy Speaker.

    The crowd had evidently been galvanised into action. Drooping shoulders and listless looks had given way to bright smiles, hugs and handshakes. It was as if the Deputy Speaker had given each member of the crowd a dose of his white powder. We continued to prepare, dividing the crowd into small groups and briefing them regarding their roles.

At six in the morning the crowd moved on foot to the large courtyard in front of the White House. Unsure what plans the adversary had to enter the National Assembly, we split the crowd in two. While one thousand men held the rear gate, two thousand were placed at the front gate as the occupying force. For now we allowed them to relax together as a group with the instruction to move into columns of a hundred once the signal was given.

The journalists started arriving before seven. The whole place was still quiet, as the workers and security men had not yet arrived. They started trickling in at about half past seven. Our plan was for the Honourable Members in our group to recede to the background and for the designated student and labour leaders to take over the show. Our duty was to bring the people to the democratic arena, a duty which we had now completed. At about eight, the Divisional Police Officer attached to the National Assembly came in the company of two other officers. He approached the crowd at the front entrance and sorted out the leaders, from whom he asked for the police permit granting them permission to carry out a demonstration. The leaders quietly, firmly and courteously informed the police officer that they did not require any permit before visiting the parliament. On being asked how they had gained access to the National Assembly, the leaders said that they had simply walked in.

The policemen left. Within thirty minutes, three lorryloads of anti-riot policemen, heralded by a siren, replaced them. As soon as the lorries came to a halt, about a hundred anti-riot policemen jumped down and surrounded the crowd, which had by then formed itself into a defensive half-circle formation following our instructions. Seeing that they could not cope with the crowd, the policemen returned to their lorries to await instructions.

Meanwhile there was confusion in the Presidency. News of the invasion of the National Assembly by the crowd had reached the President, who was beside himself with anger as he shouted obscenities at the Chief Security Adviser, who in turn summoned the Inspector General of Police. On getting back to his office at the police headquarters in Garki, the IG summoned the Commissioner of Police for the Federal Capital Territory who in turn ordered the DPO in charge of the National Assembly to investigate the matter and report to him immediately. I was in the lobby of the White House monitoring the situation when the sound of another set of sirens reached me. A few minutes later, a column of police lorries led by two armoured tanks snaked its way into the entrance of the National Assembly premises. Right behind the last police lorry were three buses full of Honourable Members belonging to the Wenike group. Their intention was to use the armoured tanks to bulldoze their way into the premises to effect the impeachment of the Speaker.

By now, the two thousand workers at the front entrance of the National Assembly had formed themselves into several columns as a human wall against the approaching policemen. Rather than panic at the sight of the armoured tanks, the crowd joined hands together and started singing solidarity songs. A band backed them up.

*We shall overcome, 2ce*
*We shall overcome some day eee.*
*Ooo, deep in my heart,*
*I do believe,*
*That we shall overcome some day.*

As the crowd sang, the armoured tanks hesitated and slowed down, stopping a few metres to the crowd. One after the other, the police lorries also came to a halt. The DPO, a short thickest man in dark-blue and black police officer's uniform, jumped down from the leading truck and climbed the leading tank. With a megaphone in his hand, he appealed to the protesters to clear the way for the legislators who he explained were going about their lawful duties in the service of the nation. "I appeal to you to please allow our lawmakers to pass after which you can continue your demonstration. I assure you that all your grievances will be looked into by the appropriate authorities."

As he finished speaking the crowd responded with a thunderous "No, no, no …"

The Commissioner of Police joined the DPO. They sought to persuade the protesters to give way but they were rebuffed again. Meanwhile, in the leading bus conveying the legislators, Hon. Wenike and his group, including the Speaker-elect Honourable Mohammed Abubakar, were getting worried.

Honourable Kasali lit a cigarette. "I said it. I said it for all to hear. I knew right within me that the Speaker and his group were up to something but nobody believed me." Turning to Wenike he said, "Leader, you should have allowed me to deal with that rat Samuel. He sabotaged all our plans."

Wenike gestured at Honourable Elizabeth. "It's not my fault. She was the one who pleaded on behalf of the randy saboteur."

Lizzy fluttered her eyelids in an ambiguous gesture. "What beats me is how this large crowd crept into the assembly premises under the nose of the security agencies."

Wenike said, "*Chei! Dem say anoder crowd dey for back entrance.*" His nervous bloodshot eyes darted about as if searching for something.

Kasali asked, "What are the mobile policemen doing? Can't they clear them?"

"Clear them?" Lizzy asked.

"With teargas, of course: they cannot hold us to ransom like this."

"Kasali, you are not serious. Even I, a lady, the elegant sizzling Lizzy, knows that teargas is useless here. How much of it, tough-man Kasali, the foremost rascal south of the Sahara, how much teargas can clear this crowd?"

Kasali drew hard on his cigarette. "This is no time for pretty talk. Let them clear them, I say."

Lizzy persisted. "If teargas is used, depending on the direction of the wind it may be blown back in our direction and we will be in the soup. They can't use teargas. Water cannon is what they should use."

"Water can or what did you say?" Kasali said.

"Water under pressure, aimed at the crowd. It is called water cannon," Lizzy replied.

Looking out from one of the first floor offices of the White House, Senator Smollet was getting jittery. The impeachment plan he had thought was watertight was crumbling fast before his eyes. The plan had been for him to stay back in the White House to welcome the lawmakers and the new Speaker. He was also to lead the Sergeant-at-Arms to his office to retrieve the mace and take it under security as the Speaker *pro tempore* was led into the chamber. Although he had arrived in his office at about seven to put finishing touches to the documents for the House session, Smollet had been unaware of the presence of the demonstrators in the Assembly premises until he heard the sound of the siren.

As he watched the singing and dancing of the demonstrators, his stomach churned. He was fearful, angry and anxious. The opponents had paralysed his plans and were rejoicing. He thought of the President, who was sure to sack him, he thought. Smollet could see that everything was at a standstill. He saw the police chiefs remonstrating with the leaders of the protesters, without effect. Meanwhile, a detachment of policemen had gone to see if the lawmakers could gain access into the National Assembly premises using the back route; but the human wall there was thick and impenetrable.

Urgent phone calls were made to the security forces to employ force to disperse the crowd. On radio and television, solidarity messages were sent to Nigerians. At one stage, masked mobile policemen began to jump from their lorries. Noise filled the air as policemen fired teargas into the crowd. Panic engulfed many of the protesters but a stampede was prevented by their leaders, who assured them that it was teargas being used, not bullets. Having recovered from their shock, the demonstrators now brought out their kerosene-soaked handkerchiefs and tied them across their noses. Some brave ones went so far as quickly retrieving the teargas canisters and hurling them back at the policemen.

Suddenly, just as Lizzy had speculated, the wind changed course and began to waft the eye-stinging and noxious fumes in the direction of the security forces. Pandemonium set in. The police, most of whom were without masks, fled to their lorries to leave the scene. The teargas fumes stung the policemen's eyes. They also reached the buses of the lawmakers. The legislators began to cough and to clutch at their teary stinging eyes. The attempt at a quick escape complicated matters. Vehicles belonging to both the legislators and the police began to drive into each other on the narrow driveway leading to the National Assembly premises. A traffic jam ensued. Confusion, frantic cries and disorder reigned.

Seeing the teargas was playing more havoc with the security men and the lawmakers than with the protesters, the commanding officer ordered a suspension of the teargas attack. It was a moment of release and mercy for the demonstrators who were beginning to run out of kerosene and who feared that their initial resolve would crumble. They leapt for joy in frenzied jubilation when they realized that the police had stopped firing teargas and were now clambering back into their lorries. The demonstrators clapped and rejoiced all the more when they realized that the police vehicles and legislators' buses had got entangled in a gridlock. The band raised a new tune; the crowd roared out its song.

In our outpost in the Speaker's foyer, the Speaker and I fell into an ecstatic embrace.

"*Mun gode Allah! Mun gode* … thank God! thank God!" was all the Speaker could say.

# CHAPTER

# 11

Watching with bewilderment the live coverage of the encounter between the demonstrators and the security forces on television, Chief Ambrose Oneya, President of the Federal Republic of Nigeria, fell into a foul mood. "We have failed, we have failed, we have failed," he muttered to himself. The lawmakers had failed to gain access to the premises of the National Assembly. And going all over the world was the broadcast of the event. What an embarrassment, the President thought. While Senator Smollet and other government officials continued to phone in reassuring reports to the President, calls coming from abroad counselled him to call a quick truce. Prominent Nigerians watching the events on international television were seeking to prevail on the President to call a ceasefire. Mindful of the implication of lawmakers forcibly taking over parliament in collusion with the law-enforcement agencies, they warned that a violent takeover of parliament would engulf him in tragic consequences. "Seek a political solution," they said.

At exactly twelve noon, after almost four hours of hostilities, the Commander of the forces invading the National Assembly gave the order to retreat. As the police vehicles and the buses conveying the legislators sneaked their way out of the front and back gates of the National Assembly, the demonstrators could be heard singing and dancing and praising God.

*O se o, o se o, o se o, Baba!*
*O se o, o se o, o se o, Baba!*
*O se o, o se o, o se o, Baba!*

In spite of the victory, we still admonished the demonstrators to keep their positions. Who knew what President Oneya and his men would do next? The demonstrators were tired and hungry but the euphoria of victory sustained them. They continued to sing and dance as the foreign and local journalists interviewed them and beamed their activities to the world at large. The international coverage continued to portray the government in a bad light all over the world.

Radio and television experts, analysts, critics and commentators spoke learnedly and at eloquent length of the Nigerian impasse. International public opinion mounted against the Presidency. The African Union called for a political solution. The United Nations Secretary-General sent an envoy to President Oneya. Overwhelmed by the weight of opinion, national and international, President Oneya bowed to the pressure. To put an end to the embarrassment, the President put a call through to the Speaker to open dialogue and ensure peace. He requested that the premises of the National Assembly be vacated and the demonstrators sent home. He further promised to support the Speaker in all his future parliamentary duties.

Knowing how foxy the President could be, the Speaker asked the demonstrators to stay in place until a written letter of assurance could be secured from the President. He also called for an immediate meeting with Wenike group with the President in attendance, with the additional request for a joint press conference after the meeting. At first, the President, on the advice of Senator Smollet and Honourable Wenike, refused to accede to the Speaker's request. The irresistible force of international opinion once again prevailed and he was compelled to accept the Speaker's terms.

Even then, the demonstrators were directed to stay on at

the Assembly premises until the meeting was over. To forge favourable terms of reconciliation for our group, we quickly organised a mini-meeting. We took one irrevocable decision: on no account would we recall the demonstrators until a duly signed document of agreement was secured.

I accompanied the Speaker and our group to the meeting at the Presidential villa. Our group had some twenty members while the Wenike group was repre-sented by ten members. Although we were happy that we had the upper hand in the deliberations, we were careful not to appear over-exuberant.

Wenike had lost his swagger. The out-dribbled master-dribbler of Nigerian politics sat forlorn, his lips twitching, his eyes a blend of despair and rage. His constant companion, Lizzy, sat beside him and I thought she winked at me. You never know with women, I thought. Lizzy was a real exponent of the 'no-permanent-friends' policy in life, as in politics. No mistaking it now, she smiled broadly at me and winked again. We sat down in our individual groups. Gone was the usual camaraderie on display at such meetings. Everybody was a little tense.

Senator Smollet sat in a corner of the room, his head in his hands, looking very much like a dazzling striker who at the peak of his soccer career has just missed a crucial last-minute penalty shot. Smollet was out. I was sure Oneya would vent the spleen of battle defeat on him and a few other political expendables. Smollet exchanged words once or twice with Wenike. Five more members of our group, including the Deputy Speaker, came in and joined us. The DS looked cocaine-bright as he shook hands warmly with us before moving over to greet the Wenikes. He continued to chat to them until they thawed, brightened up and found themselves glad-handing and backslapping the DS. I suddenly wondered whether the President used something and what that thing was. As I was thus occupied, the President breezed into the hall in company of some of his ministers and aides. We all stood until he took his seat. His smile was forced, his bearing stiff. What does he take? I wondered. Whatever it was, it was not sufficient to mask his sullenness.

The opening prayers were said. We were then asked to introduce ourselves. As I took my turn, the President gave me the sharp glance a clergyman would give a member of the congregation who has just shouted a solidarity No! at a crucial moment in the delivery of the weekly sermon. The glance said," *You, you put sand in our gari and dust in our cornflakes. We shall get you yet.*" The protocol man called on the President to make his opening remarks. After a few perfunctory remarks, the President stated that he was never in any way part of the plan to impeach the Speaker. "As the President of the whole country and the son of … no, excuse me, and as a committed democrat, it is my bound duty to evince transparent and unshakable neutrality in such matters. In addition, I am supposed to be a good example to everybody."

Members of the Speaker's group smiled and exchanged looks that said, "We know a lie when we hear one."

Expressing his intense displeasure at how the incident had shown the country in a bad light in the comity of nations, the President said he did not want a protracted meeting. He said his first request was that the Speaker should ensure the immediate evacuation of the demonstrators from the premises of the National Assembly. Second, as the issue of the appointment of the committee chairman was the immediate cause of the crisis, the Speaker should review the exercise as a matter of urgency. The Wenike group would reciprocate the gesture by dropping the threat of impeachment, returning the mace to the House to hasten a return to plenary where other contentious issues could be adequately tackled.

The Speaker was then asked for his remarks. Following the script we had designed for his talk at our mini-meeting, the Speaker regretted the involvement of the President in the whole sordid affair. He supplied evidence to prove that the President was deeply involved in the plot to impeach him. He talked of secret recordings and photographs of the President's conversation with Senator Smollet as well as photocopies of letters between the Presidency and the Wenike group. The Speaker completed his evidence of the President's massive involvement with reference to the massive security support given to the Wenike group during the aborted invasion of National Assembly premises.

As for the evacuation of the demonstrators from the premises of the National Assembly and the review of the appointment of the committee chairmen, the Speaker declined to attend to either request until such time as the Wenike group returned the mace, along with a letter promising to desist from plunging the parliament into further crisis. Wenike, the self-declared master planner and veteran of impeachment plots, spoke next. His whole mien was listless, the bearing of a man forced to eat *eba* without meat. He spoke slowly and clumsily but his words were freighted with fierceness.

He accused the Speaker and his group of painting Nigeria in a bad light in the eyes of the whole world. He demanded that the Speaker should vacate his office for the sake of peace; at which point Lizzy hissed. He insisted that since his group still had the mace, the House could not resume its legislative activities until his group's demands were met. The discussion then became rowdy. Voices were raised and tempers flared. After some three hours, a settlement was reached. The Speaker agreed to evacuate the protesters from the premises of the Assembly that evening, but only after the Wenike group returned the mace to its rightful place. In addition, government had to give an undertaking that it would in no way victimise any of the demonstrators, whether students or workers. He agreed to review committee chairmanships and concede a few choice positions to the Wenike group. The terms were reiterated at a press conference, carried live by the media, national and international, that later took place in the Presidential Villa press centre.

Immediately after the press conference, I accom-panied the

Deputy Speaker to the National Assembly, where we addressed the protesters, lauding their courage, commitment and patriotism and thanking them for rising to the occasion when summoned. The Deputy Speaker in addition assured them that their names would be written in gold when the history of democracy was written.

"Compatriots," the Deputy Speaker said, "Today you have established beyond all doubts the power of the people, their collective will and wisdom, moulded and merged together in synchronized movement, is indeed mightier than the guns of tyranny and the tanks of oppression. This day from Magoro to Maiduguri, from Lagos to Langtang, from Nnewi to Kaura Namoda, up the Adamawa Plateau and down the valley of the Niger Delta, you have, by your staunch opposition to a conniving captain-of-state and his conspiratorial minions, restored hope and confidence to millions of Nigerians and re-established the truth now ringing all over the world that there is hope for the black man. No more the national slur on our youth as cocaine-inhaling cultists and scammers; no more the arrogant description of you our youth as drug and child traffickers. This parliament will erect a plaque that will symbolise today's victory at this very site where the battle against nepotism, avarice and totalitarianism was bitterly fought and masterfully won …" And so on.

# CHAPTER 12

Evening came. The rain had just stopped and the queen-of-the-night flowers lining the front of my flat began to exude a beautiful, tantalizing fragrance. The June twilight, the smell of rain, the tender greenery, the droning of insects, the stillness and warmth – all these seemed new and in some way unusual against the backdrop of the day's events. Overwhelmed by the euphoria of our victory and the stress of the last few hours, I went straight to bed.

I was awakened at about a quarter to two by the persistent ringing of my mobile phone. It was my sister Maria in the UK. In an emotion-laden voice, she told me how she had just rushed Mark, my six year old son, to hospital with a stomach ache. Mark had been living with Maria for the past four years since Agnes and I had separated.

"I thought it was a mild thing, when he first complained," Maria said. "I thought maybe he had overeaten or was constipated. So I gave him some antacids but the pain got worse. I had to call an ambulance when he started throwing up. The doctor thinks it is appendicitis. They will need to operate on him as soon as possible."

Fear gripped me. Surgery on my six-year-old-son Mark? … Oh, help me, God! I said quietly in prayer. Handsome Mark, his chubby face and cherubic smile a replica of his mother's good looks. My sweet darling Mark. I had seen him last two years ago when Maria came to Nigeria on vacation with her husband, a diplomat, and their daughters. They spent two weeks, but I had had only two days to spend with my son, so intense, so vigorous and time-consuming was the electioneering campaign. To make up for it all, I promised Maria I would fly over to the UK on a visit. I could not fulfil the thrice-renewed promise and now came the terrible news that Mark was going under the knife.

"Can't the doctors try drugs? Must it be an operation?" I asked.

"Sam, you should know now. Surgery is the only solution. It's a routine operation."

"Did you call Agnes?" I asked.

"Oh yes, but I did not get a reply. Should I try again?"

"Don't worry, Maria. How are Amanda and Cecilia? And their ever travelling Daddy?"

"We all are well," Maria answered.

"Don't bother Agnes. I will come over. I got a visa late last year for one of my unfulfilled visits."

The Speaker, when I approached him, was not going to allow me to travel. "Sam, don't even try to convince me. At this trying period when all hands, especially yours, must be on deck?"

"But it's my son. The doctors are operating on him. He is only six."

"I am deeply sorry, Sam. You should have told me that. I thought you were trying to get away from it all for a long weekend with Sally."

I interrupted. "You mean Lizzy?"

"Oh well, when is your flight? In what way can I be of help?" he asked, opening the safe behind his desk, counting out a wad of dollars and handing them over to me. "Sam, I am sorry, I don't have sterling. Do manage this."

"*Na gode Ranka ya dade, Allah ya saka da alheri* ... thank you sir. May the good Lord continue to bless you," I gushed in appreciation.

Although I had visited the United States, China and Cuba, I had never been to the United Kingdom. I was therefore nervous as I boarded the British Airways plane at Abuja the evening after I received my sister's call. I had received another call from her telling me the surgery was over and that Mark was in stable condition. Maria told me she had got in touch with Agnes at last. Agnes had remarried and was resident in Lagos. Agnes had apologised she could not come because she didn't have a British visa but was relieved I would be in UK to hold our son's hand as he recuperated. It must have been the fatigue of the past few days' activities: as soon as dinner was served on the plane, I fell asleep and apparently slept throughout the flight. A hostess woke me to fasten my seat belt in preparation for landing. A few minutes later, at Heathrow's Terminal Five, I pulled out the piece of paper on which I had written my sister's address: No. 45 Kemsing Gardens, Canterbury, Kent.

The pilot had asked us to get our travel documents ready as the immigration officials were already at the aircraft door to inspect us. To my great annoyance, just a few metres outside the plane, two officials, one holding a dog on a leash, asked me to kindly step aside for questioning. Why, I did not know. Also most embarrassing was their request that I should place my hand luggage on the floor for the dog to sniff. The ugly brute lacked all interest in my luggage and me, but rather lunged for one corpulent woman's luggage, wagging its tail furiously.

It was about six in the morning. I was free of immigration hassles but still had a two-hour journey to make to Kent. The prevailing order at Heathrow Airport was a delight to my eyes. I thought of Murtala Mohammed Airport and wished we could have it better. Everybody seemed to be in a hurry, moving determinedly. I looked round for the information desk. Maria had assured me I would get assistance there on how to reach Canterbury. I found my mind going back decades in recollection of lessons with Mr. Olujimi, my form two History teacher, who told us that Canterbury was of great historical significance. It had a Cathedral, an archbishop and had been made famous in literature by Geoffrey Chaucer: all this I could remember, but nothing more of Olujimi's stirring history lessons in my old mission high school could be summoned from the mists of memory.

A blonde greeted me with a pleasant smile as I approached the information desk. In my eagerness I virtually shoved the piece of paper under her nose. She took a look and said, "You have quite a journey ahead of you, but first you must get to Victoria Station in central London." She assisted me in obtaining an underground rail ticket and gave me a tube map of the London Underground. The journey from Heathrow to Victoria lasted about an hour and half. The train was so congested I had to squeeze myself into the coach.

At Victoria I had to buy another ticket for the Virgin train to Canterbury. As it crawled out of the bustling Victoria Station, a beautiful vista unfolded of the English countryside with its rolling green acres and browsing fat cows. Lovely sheep grazed in the paddocks between Rochester and Chatham. Horses galloped over the hills and valleys while swans swam on the placid lakes.

I was brought out of my reverie by a PA announcement: the train would split in two at Gillingham Station. Only the front four coaches would continue to Canterbury. A quick check confirmed that I was in coach seven, meaning that I was in the wrong section of the train and if I did not move in time, I would end up in Dover Priory.

Quickly grabbing my bags, I hurried out of coach seven to the front four coaches. Fortunately, I found a seat in coach four before the train was split. I was adjusting myself on the seat when a man tapped me on the shoulder. I looked up into the eyes of a tall uniformed gentleman asking for my ticket. I obliged him. Twilight came. I looked out through the window. A field full of already-cut bales of wheat ready for the market greeted my eyes. I remembered my father's farm in Kachia and the millet at harvest – all so similar. The one difference was that the bales of wheat were cut neatly as if machine-measured.

I dozed off. Some twenty minutes later my destination was announced, Canterbury East. I called Maria from a pay phone at the station and she turned up a few minutes later in a three-door Ford Focus. I noticed wryly that she had put on some flesh since we saw each other last two years earlier. She urged me to first go home to freshen up but I insisted on seeing Mark before anything else. "The operation is over. He is OK," Maria told me.

"I won't be able to relax until I see Mark," I replied.

Maria told me the hospital was a twenty-minute drive from the station. During the short trip I studied Canterbury, obviously a town with a lot of history behind it. I saw its famous walls, which historians say protected it from siege by the Romans, and the famous cathedral. I faintly hoped that the Archbishop would pop up within my view. We soon arrived at the Kent and Canterbury Hospital on Ethelbert Road.

The hospital was a lovely red-brick building set against a well-landscaped compound. We got to the children's ward. Mark lay quietly in bed with two drips attached to his arms. Excitedly I called out his name. He emerged from sleep, turned slowly towards me and opened his eyes in bewilderment, seemingly attempting to make out who I was.

"It's Daddy, Mark," I declared softly to my son.

He looked passively at me, showing no evidence of recognition. My heart sank. I moved closer and touching his head, said "Mark, daddy. It's me, your Daddy." Another long bewildered look. I wondered. Was my only child, the son of my loins, rejecting me? Tears welled up in my eyes. Maria sought to help. "Mark," she said," Look! It's your Daddy. He came all the way from Nigeria to see you." Mark continued to stare at the wall with a numbing blank stare. It was a hopeless moment. I went to the balcony, sighing heavily. Maria joined me moments later. "Samuel, it's all right. He's only a child. You have to give him time. Remember he saw you last two years ago and for a mere two days!"

I smiled nervously. "You know this is what I keep saying about politics. Family members are the sufferers, the wives, the girlfriends, the children who don't see Daddy as often as they want. A crying shame: how can my son consider me a stranger?" Maria broke in reassuring me that before the end of my five-day visits, Mark would warm up marvellously to me. It was not to be. Sadly, when I left Canterbury for Nigeria at the end of my five-day visit, Mark was still a perfect stranger to me, cold unyielding, almost hostile.

\* \* \*

I was welcomed back to Abuja by a thunderstorm that started as soon as I left Nnamdi Azikiwe International Airport. By the time I reached my flat in Apo, the rain had become a torrential downpour accompanied by a prolonged rumbling thunder, dull at first then roaring and crackling so violently that the glass in the windows tinkled. I went to the window and leaned my head against the pane. The storm outside was going on with an intense beauty. The lightning flashed on the right and then on the left of the house. Suddenly, the lights in my apartment blinked and finally spluttered out.

I lit two candles and tried to see if I could close the windows to reduce the incoming draught. The flat was empty and lonely. I felt empty. The encounter with my son was a pain that would not go away. There was a void in my life that being a busy patriotic parliamen-tarian could not fill. Deep inside me an ache had begun, an ache that gained a sharp edge whenever I ran into my colleagues hand-in-hand with their wives and surrounded by their children. It was that ache that I had felt at the hospital in Canterbury when my son, Mark, turned his face away from me.

The thought began to form in my heart that Agnes was to blame for leaving me. And where was she? In another man's house, of course. If I went to her on bended knees, perhaps she would yield her heart to my plea for forgiveness. Could I make up for all the pain I caused her when she was with me? Well, then. Now my thoughts gravitated towards dinner. I checked the freezer; inside it was a frozen pot of chicken stew my girlfriend, the nurse, had kept for me. As I held the cold pot in my hands, the thought of going to all the trouble of warming it overwhelmed me. I put it back in the freezer, feeling well and truly nostalgic for Agnes and her culinary prowess. I remembered the aroma of good cooking that filled our house and how like a king at a feast I felt walking majestically to the table to tackle Agnes's delicious food. But the worst of it all was the loneliness. My bed had become an arctic outpost fit only for penguins. My mind surveyed the past … if only Lizzy had accepted my proposition, if only Agnes had not left me … if only … but right inside me I knew no one else was to be blamed. I was responsible for my troubles. My needs gnawed at my insides and they were increasingly difficult to ignore.

# CHAPTER

# 13

I found the Speaker stretched out on a garden chair at the back of his official residence in the Apo Quarters. In his hand was Barack Obama's bestseller *The Audacity of Hope*. His calm and relaxed face broke into a deep smile that touched both corners of his mouth as soon as he saw me. "How was your trip? How is your son?" he asked as soon as I got to his side.

"Everything is now OK. I am also glad to see you so relaxed," I said. "I hope those chaps kept to the terms of our agreement?"

"O yes, they did ... *alhamdu lillah* ... thank God. In fact, their co-operation is commendable. They were battle-weary, fagged out, tired of fighting us. You know what I did?"

"What?" I asked.

"They asked for four Grade A Committees. I gave them, guess how many?"

"Two," I said, remembering at that moment for no reason in particular the four coaches split in two on the way to Canterbury.

The Speaker fairly jumped out of the garden chair to pat me on the back affectionately. "Sam, you think just like me. I gave them, yes just two: Agriculture and Education. I kept the others as they were."

"What about the NNDC committee that was the bone of contention?"

"Sam, you want to know everything all at once. I did what you would have done. I asked myself, what will Clausewitz do in this situation?"

"He wouldn't shift an inch," I cut in.

"Yes, I refused, Sam, to concede the NNDC chairmanship. Don't give your rivals too much strength. Well, in the alternative I added four Grade B committees to the list. Next question, inquisitive Sam. By the way, what will you drink?"

The Speaker called one of his assistants to bring me wine and get him his briefcase. I asked: "Has the President called again as he promised?"

"He is a changed man. He has undergone, what is this term in biology about insects?"

"Complete metamorphosis."

"Trust Sam to help out. President Oneya has undergone a complete metamorphosis. He has, believe it or not, called me every day since that day we met in the Villa. He has even promised to come and see me at home one of these days."

I frowned.

The Speaker was quick to notice. "The wine not your taste or something, Sam?" he asked.

"Not the wine, Mr. Speaker, but the President. A leopard never changes its spots. I don't believe President Oneya has changed, is changing or can change. *Kare ne shi, sanye da fatar rago* ... he is a fox in a sheep's skin."

"A good politician must be flexible. Oneya was shocked at the publicity we gave that demonstration in the National Assembly; it really jolted him, he confessed. He said he never expected it. He is yet to recover from the negative publicity the project gave his office. Oneya is a good politician, clever and flexible. I believe ... what I believe he is trying to do is affect a complete rapprochement with us," the Speaker said.

I took a sip of the sparkling French wine, smacking my lips in satisfaction. "Hm ... hm," I began," if I were you I would not be too relaxed yet. Mr. Speaker, you are a good and flexible politician. I guess I am a good and flexible politician as well. Well, mark my words, President Oneya is a fox, a crafty smiling deceiver; one moment he is kissing you, the next he is stabbing you in the back."

The Speaker smiled. "You will soon change your mind. Hen, hen, Sam, I have some news for you. Good news, of course."

I wagged my finger. "Have you made me a Committee Chairman?"

"Wrong guess this time. Your time will come, Sam. You are a potential Speaker, I tell you." The Speaker rummaged in his briefcase for a while, finally bringing out a sheaf of papers that he handed over to me. "I got them yesterday," he said. "It's a Lagos seminar, sorry, Workshop on Conflict Resolution. It's for Wednesday, Thursday and Friday next week. Sam, you will have to attend the workshop."

"Oh yes, oh yes. I can see the Baba Kura paper."

"Yes, Sam. Please read out the titles again."

"*Conflicts Between Pastoralists and Agriculturalists in North-eastern Nigeria: Theories, Perspectives and Solutions, by Professor Baba Kura.*"

"Quite a mouthful, Sam but all he is saying is …"

"That Fulani herdsmen and Kachia farmers should resolve their conflicts. I will be there. There is also …"

"Oh, the Albert paper …"

"Mr. Speaker, you have gone through it all."

"You know, Sam, I find reading on and off the job a pleasure. Please read Albert's title."

"*Conflict management and Peace-Making Initiatives in Kaduna State,*" I read.

"Yes, my dear Sam. Your Bill will have academic backbone. Those two papers will be a real help. Make sure you talk with Professor …"

"Baba Kura and yes, Professor Olawale Albert. I will pick their brains."

"Lagos is a rowdy, glamorous place, Sam. Don't get distracted by the city girls."

"I hate HIV/AIDS. This is no time for playing the field. In fact, those papers will form a very important background… a useful framework to the Bill on resolving the perennial conflicts between the Kachia farmers and the Fulani cattle rearers."

The Speaker smiled. "It is a top-priority Bill. We shall give it urgent consideration. Well, you have your work cut out. You will attend the Lagos workshop. You will draft the Bill. Then, this is very important … we shall organise a public hearing to which representatives of the farmers and cattle rearers will be invited. As I always say, it is elementary and excellent democratic practice to listen to both sides to obtain a picture of the problem."

I spread my hands wide, saying, "I appreciate the scope of preparation for the Bill. The issue of getting the representatives of the farmers will not be difficult. My problem is how to reach the Fulanis. Ever on the move and they can hardly bear to be separated from their cattle to attend meetings."

The Speaker laughed. "Who gave you that fable? You've forgotten that I am a full-blooded Fulani and ever proud of the fact. No, we are not a difficult people. It won't be difficult getting across to the herdsmen. I will personally see to that."

The level of the wine in the bottle had gone down a whole lot. I checked the time on my mobile phone furtively, not wanting to return to the crippling desolation of my lonely flat. The Speaker caught the gesture but misread it. "You want to be on your way. Jetlag and all that. Ah, it's ten o'clock. It has been time well spent, Sam."

I said goodnight. As the Speaker was about to see me off, his phone rang and I excused myself. At the Speaker's gate I had to stop for a moment for a grey Range Rover to pass. As it did, I instinctively looked up. A sigh escaped my lips. At the wheel was a very familiar face – the President of the Federal Republic of Nigeria.

\* \* \*

Relaxed and at peace with the world as he reclined on his garden chair, the Speaker was shocked to hear his Personal Assistant announce the arrival of the President. The President had truly said he would be paying him a visit but he had rather doubted him.

"My dear Speaker," the tall gangling President boomed in his baritone voice as he extended his hand. The President wore a well-tailored safari suit with a bowler hat popularly called "Resource Control" among his people in the South-South geo-political Zone.

"Your Excellency, shall we go in?"

"Oh, no my dear Speaker. Not at all. Let me enjoy the atmosphere here. It is cool and sedate."

In moments, a trolley laden with assorted snacks and drinks was wheeled to the poolside. After further exchange of pleasantries, the discussion went from one general issue to another. The President poured some Chateau Talbot '78 into a glass full of ice. He took a sip and beamed as his host returned from the bar with two crystal glasses and a large bottle of cognac on a silver tray.

"Tell me," the President said, "Mr. Speaker, what are your plans for the elections coming up in two year's time? Are you thinking of becoming a Senator? We need good people to keep up the good work. People like you."

The Speaker, ever the cautious politician, refused to commit himself. He said he would, as a good party man, do whatever the party wanted him to do.

"Perhaps, my dear Speaker, we could get you into the Governor's lodge at Maiduguri? How about that?" the President said, laughing. It was obvious that the liquor was already taking its effect just as the Speaker wanted. The whole country knew of the President's weakness for women and also of his partiality for good strong liquor. Having finished the glass of Chateau Talbot, the President now turned his attention to the cognac, from which he poured a portion into a large glass. He added two ice cubes. Without waiting for the Speaker to answer his question he went on.

"It is my belief, Mr. Speaker that we had better start now. The early bird catches the worm. Time and tide wait for no man. We had better start working for the next election lest in two years' time we bite our fingers in bitter regret. The opposition is already at work luring our members to their side. I think we need to start our campaign very early."

"You are right, Your Excellency. We need to widen our very narrow majority in the House."

The President took a sip from his cognac. He allowed the warmth of the alcohol to course through his veins before he continued speaking.

"You see, many people are blinded to the fact that our democracy is … is … like … a premature baby. It needs intensive care, incubation, nurturing. Yes, our fledging, nascent democracy needs serious attention. A prime factor here is the need to ensure continuity. Yes, e, eh … Yes …where was I? Strong. I like this cognac – strong. For a strong democracy … continuity is the word. Continuity, Mr. Speaker, are you with me?"

Wondering where Oneya was headed, the Speaker nodded.

"You see, the opposite of continuity is not change. It is discontinuity, instability, chaos. But we want continuity, stability, order and peace. Even political scientists know that a rapid change of government can disrupt things. A term is four years, all right. But you and I know it takes that number of years just for a government to settle down."

The President paused for a sip of his strong drink. He continued. "The Americans have it right. They give their Presidents eight years, mostly. Four years to settle down. Four years to start working. But America is developed. We are not developed. Mr. Speaker, what I am saying is that … well, you know, as a responsible and far-sighted Leader …eight years in office preparing and incubating our democracy for the future. Most Nigerians want continuity. Read the papers. Watch television news analysts. Listen to radio reports on national politics. And keep your ear to the ground, as a good grassroots politician. Add everything together; what do you get? Rather than change the current government, the position of many Nigerians is that we good people should continue the good work for a good four more years. We shall remain in office for another term. *Vox populi, vox dei*. The voice of the people is the voice of God. Mr. Speaker, did you take Latin in School?'

"In 1962 ..."

No, no, the future is what we are talking about now. Mr. Speaker ..." the President said, pointing to the near-empty bottle of Cognac.

"Yes, more ..." the Speaker started.

The President beamed," You mean you agree ..."

The Speaker demurred.

"Oh, I meant cognac."

The Speaker signalled his aides. "Your Excellency, you will be rounding up your eight-year two-term tenure in two years' time. The question will surely be asked: on what basis do you want to remain in office?"

"Oh, yes, yes," the President said, welcoming a fresh tray of his favourite drink. "I was coming to that; but before that let me just say something." The President leaned across to the Speaker, who could smell his guest's alcohol-laden breath. He said, "Time. We need more time to execute our party's manifesto. How can we leave at this stage? How can we leave with several uncompleted projects? The opposition will rubbish us. I also want you to know, my dear Speaker, that we shall all be beneficiaries of the continuity agenda if it sails through." The President paused for a swig of his cognac.

"As a matter of fact, people like you who have been very good to the party can be kicked upstairs, as I said, to Governor's lodge in Borno State. I have gone to this length just to let you realize how important this project is. Are you with me thus far?"

The Speaker nodded.

"Now to your question, my dear Speaker, how do we hope to remain in office? This, as you know, can be achieved only by a constitutional amendment. This is where you will be very useful, my dear Speaker, as the Bill has to be passed by the National Assembly."

As the President paused to take another sip of cognac, the stillness of the atmosphere was so intense that the sound of a cricket passing sounded like that of an aircraft flying overhead.

That was when the Speaker spoke. "It will be difficult to dribble our way through, Mr. President. Where do I start? The press will scream blue murder the moment they hear of a constitutional amendment designed to lengthen your tenure."

The President belched. "Forget the press. They are a bunch of irrelevant noisemakers."

"Mr. President," the Speaker continued, "those in the North believe the Presidency is their due now. It is their turn. And they are right. They will launch maximum battle against any force, movement, personality or amendment that wants to deny them the Presidency. They will not agree. They will stir up things. They will work up a storm …"

The President nodded. "Go on, Mr. Speaker, go on."

"Other politicians, who believe rightly or wrongly that a return of the current political leaders to power will constitute a problem for their own political ambitions, will set the polity on fire," the Speaker said.

"In that case, it will be fire for fire," the President said.

The Speaker continued. "In short, Mr. President, we need to rethink this whole constitutional amend-ment plan. It will be mighty hard to fight through." The two political leaders continued to talk. They talked far into the night.

# CHAPTER 14

The Master of Ceremonies was inviting some dignitaries to the high table when I arrived at the Conference Hall of the Lagos Sheraton, venue of the two-day workshop on Conflict Management and Peace-Making Initiatives. I was quickly recognised and, much to my chagrin, hauled to the high table as the representative of the Speaker. I had looked forward to sitting in the midst of the participants to hobnob with the eggheads, network with the NGO personnel and accost the media men. Now I had no choice but to go up and sit with the other dignitaries on the exalted table.

Soon, I was called upon to deliver the opening address on the Speaker's behalf. The Speaker's passionate concern for a cessation to the long and embarrassing history of conflict between pastoralists and agriculturalists came across vividly. As the Speaker concluded:

"The recent practice of forcing Fulani pastoralists to move after decades of settlement in a location could lead to violent conflicts. The Fulani have ceaselessly complained that in places where they were allowed to settle, they were made to understand that they had no rights to land. In short, they were living on borrowed land for a borrowed period of time. It was expected that as pressure on land increased, the Fulani agro-pastoralists and their landlords would be locked in a life-and-death struggle to resolve the land issue. If this new wave of conflicts is to be avoided, fresh initiatives – set within the framework of the Land Use Decree of 1978 allowing customary rights over land, including grazing reserves – will be needed from the traditional and state institutions on the ground."

Applause greeted the Speaker's conclusion, which was that the National Assembly was planning to enact appropriate legislation to safeguard the rights of both pastoralists and agriculturalists and hence, put an end to their incessant conflicts. It was his belief that although the remote cause of the dispute between the two groups was basically economic, the trend, if unchecked, could spread to other parts of the country, and eventually degenerate to a national crisis threatening the demo-cratic process.

Furthermore, the Speaker promised to bring many of the intellectuals at the conference into the bill-making process as resource persons at the soon-to-be-held public hearing of the Bill.

\* \* \*

The Speaker's passion for the Bill did not abate. Entitled: A Bill For An Act To Establish A Commission For Pastoralists and Agriculturists In The Federal Republic Of Nigeria, it sailed through the first and second readings at a rapid clip with a mere two weeks separating the readings. I was the lead sponsor for the Bill; twelve other members were its co-sponsors. In preparation for the public hearing we decided to link up with the relevant stakeholders including leaders of farmers, cattle rearers, butchers, community leaders and the law enforcement agencies.

In view of the many-sidedness of the project, different members were assigned to different stakeholders. My assignment was to link up with the farmers and the Fulani cattle rearers. My antecedents with the farmers were a big help; it was quite easy for me to get across to the farmers through the Association of Nigerian Farmers. The farmers, elated that their dire plight had finally come to the front burner of legislative activity, promised to attend the event in large numbers. Linking up with the Fulani cattle rearers was also not too difficult. I was able to reach their leaders through their association called *Miyetti Allah* (we thank God). Also, the Speaker, a Fulani himself, had, as he had earlier promised, contacted his kith and kin. Even then, the Fulani leaders took me to their settlement called *riga* and introduced me and my project to the community leader called *ardo* while my colleague, Hon. Baba Muhammed, acted as an interpreter.

My last port of call and perhaps the most challenging of my visits was to a *riga* on the Bauchi-Jos highway. Because of the recent skirmishes between the native Christians and the settler Hausa/Fulanis, tension was still high when I visited the settlement, a *riga* called Naborda, one weekend. My visit fell, happily, on a market day. The gaily-dressed Fulani moved merrily all over the place. Young men – to my intense surprise – wore braided hair, lipstick, earrings and arm bangles. A friend whom I told of this later termed it "the feminisation of Fulani males". So feminine was the garb of the young men that it was difficult to differentiate them from the girls. The young men favoured very tight trousers. On their heads were brightly-coloured headscarves, on top of which they placed English hats at seductive angles. Underneath their short and shining tunics were neat T-shirts. Sun-spectacles of all kinds were on view. On their feet were canvas shoes and in their hands a long, strong and stout stick called *sanda*.

On enquiry, I was told that the *sanda* was both a weapon and a cultural item. It looks feeble, but *sanda* is really a lethal weapon. Handled by an expert user, it can break a leg, immobilise an aggressive animal and even crack a human skull. As I held the *sanda* in my hands, my mind went to the several encounters we had had with the deadly weapon during the regular invasion of our family farm by the Fulani cattle rearers. Most of the Fulani men also carried radios on their shoulders, from which loud music and regular news blared.

More fascinating than the male Fulanis were the females. They moved gracefully. Their clothes were also brightly coloured.

Set against their brown complexions, these clothes gave them a wonderful charm. While some stayed home for housekeeping duties, the others took their ware – fresh milk, yoghurt, beads and trinkets – to the market. One particular girl caught my attention. She could not have been more than nineteen years old. Slender, she had wide eyes and walked as if she did not quite touch the ground. She swung her wide hips gracefully and effortlessly, a milk gourd on her head, her hands by her sides. Her long, silky black hair cascaded down her shoulders in a beautiful Fulani braid generously decorated with beads of many colours. Most delightful of all was her pointed nose and sonorous voice, which pealed out in the bucolic settlement as she played with her friends.

I named her "the red girl", as almost everything she wore was red. Even the beads in her woven hair were red. I was intrigued to see that some of the young Fulani maidens carried radios. I laughed when my escort explained this:

"The radios are a sign that the girls have been betrothed to the men who own them. You will also have noted that some Fulani men have tied scarves on their heads. Those scarves belong to the ladies to whom they are romantically linked. The radio and the scarf are therefore mating symbols. Their message: 'Keep off, I am already booked.'" I quickly checked on the red girl – why, I don't know – but she was booked. I felt very sad for some unknown reason.

We moved round and got to a thick green bushy area. Smoke billowed upwards from a small clearing in the thick vegetation. Moving closer, I could make out the *bukkas* standing in their round thatched walls and roofs. Fire burned brightly beneath a pot placed on a tripod of stones. Three women sat by the fire in front of their brown thatched huts with its natural green walls. They were clad in embroidered hand-woven wrapper, dress and headgear, all white.

Outside in the open field, ladies in multi-coloured fabrics chatted gaily as they expertly pounded millet in mortars. A few metres away from where the girls worked, a cow that had just delivered a calf grazed languidly in a patch of grass behind the *bukka*. The environment was peaceful, pastoral, and deeply restful for me; a sweet contrast to the bustling life of Abuja that I was used to. As previously arranged, the leaders of the Fulani community gathered at the centre of their settlement for the meeting. There and then, I told them of the proposed bill which it was hoped would settle once and for all their longstanding feud with the farmers.

The Fulanis surveyed me warily, answered my questions tersely and held their bodies rigidly. They saw me as a stranger and wondered at my motives. However, when my colleague, Honourable Baba Mohammed, a Fulani, came and talked to them, they warmed to me. They thanked me for my sponsorship of a Bill to put an end to their clashes with the farmers.

Alhaji Musa Adamu, the *ardo* Fulani said, "Allah be praised! Any time we had a clash, government blamed us, blamed us, blamed us; now they will know the truth." He pulled thoughtfully at his white beard.

Another elderly man spoke. "The farmers are equally guilty of provoking us. *Haba*, with their eyes wide open, they will begin to farm on lands traditionally set apart for grazing."

On how to stop the perennial clashes, the Fulanis asked for *brutali,* a north-south corridor of land reserved for grazing. This according to them had to be owned and protected by the Federal Government. They were astute enough to incorporate a request for regular and cheap livestock vaccines in their demands. They argued that through the provision of regular dairy products and supply of meat protein they were significant stakeholders in the country's economy. In addition, they also paid their taxes.

"We need to be protected. Government should protect us. And help our children. We need schools, nomadic schools for our children. Once educated, our children will be very useful to society," their leader declared.

I advised them to put their grievances, demands, observations and recommendations in writing and to send these to my Committee in readiness for the much-awaited public hearing coming up soon. For some reason, my comments sparked off a buzz of excited talk. The worry was how to get the writing done. Nearly all their literate children had left the *riga* for the cities. One of them suddenly remembered a young girl in the village sufficiently literate to help them out.

She was sent for by the elders and I was a little startled looking up to see that it was my "red" girl who was going to be their amanuensis. Easy on the eyes at a distance, she was at close range an indisputable beauty. I gazed unabashedly at her delicate well-proportioned hips as she sauntered towards us. Tall and light-complexioned, she wore a bright yellow wrapper, red brassiere and braided hair decorated with lots of brightly coloured beads. She had large red earrings, a red handbag and a small red transistor set.

She was asked to come and sit by me so I could dictate certain facts to her. As she did, I caught a whiff of her powerful fragrance. Her pointed nose and thin lips suggested a Caucasian provenance. I read somewhere that the Fulani are in fact an international race, probably because of their nomadic nature. In Europe they are known as gypsies, while in Africa they are everywhere. Suddenly the girl's voice brought me back. She told me her name was Batejo, which in her native Fulfulde meant 'red girl'. She had learnt to speak, read and write English at a nearby nomadic school in the area. She also told me she helped her mother in her milk trade as a milkmaid. I gave her a few pieces of paper and a pen to record the minutes of the meeting.

The Fulani of Nabordo spoke and spoke, pouring out their hearts in a litany of grievances. Their leader, the Seriki Fulani, Alhaji Adamu, expressed their anger and bitterness at what he considered their neglect by their elected leaders. His voice reached a high pitch. "All they wanted is our votes. Those politicians. Vote for us! Have a good life! Vote for us! Milk and honey will flow! But once they are voted in, they become deaf and dumb to our plight … you wouldn't even see them … only civil servants hunting us all over for cattle tax! Then the crooked vet doctors who bleed and bleed us of money before vaccinating our cattle. Let politicians leave us alone! No more taxes! No more votes! If anybody comes here to canvass for votes …"

"We shall stone them!" the rest of them screamed.

The meeting was an eye-opener. I had not guessed the Fulani were so hard done by. The animosity I had harboured against them over the decades vanished. They were a people beset with troubles and oppressed by the authorities. Little wonder they were so aggres-sive. As the Fulani elder restated the issues they wanted me to capture in the proposed Bill, Batejo and I, working together, set them in order on paper. Her English was good and her handsome handwriting a fitting complement to her beauty.

"Batejo," I asked her, "why did you stop schooling?"

"I would have loved to continue my education but my parents withdrew me in preparation for marriage," she explained. "I love books. I enjoy reading, but there are no libraries in this locality. Not even bookshops."

"Oh, that," I said." I will get you one or two books."

We were putting finishing touches to our work when a young Fulani man came over to us. Batejo looked up and smiled, saying," My husband-to-be."

"Husband-to-be? Are you already betrothed?"

"Yes, last year. I am carrying his radio and he is wearing my scarf."

I looked up at the man. Tied to his jet-black braided hair was a red scarf. Two large earrings dangled from his lobes. He wore a permanent smile, a tight-fitting red shirt, knee-length white stockings and black rubber shoes. His oversized sun-spectacles gave him the air of a fun-loving young man. He had not been with us a minute when two other young men joined him, similarly dressed and holding tenaciously to their *sandas* as if their lives depended on them.

"What is your name?" I asked in all innocence.

Batejo said," He does not speak English. His name is Gidado."

"What does Gidado mean?" I asked.

"It means, 'the beloved'."

At the mention of his name, Gidado smiled proudly and readjusted his sunglasses. He pointed to his friends, one after the other and said, "Aliyu, Bello."

I shook hands with them. "How old is Gidado?" I asked.

"Twenty," Batejo answered.

"How come he can't speak English?"

Batejo explained. "His father refused to send him to school, told him to follow the cattle instead."

"So what does he do now?"

"He still follows the cattle. Sometimes he returns the same day. And sometimes he is gone for days."

"Don't' you miss him?"

"Yes, but what can I do? He has to work more and more to get enough cows to marry me."

"How many cows are your parents asking for?"

"Eight," Batejo replied, smiling.

"How many does he have now?"

"Five."

I smiled at Gidado. Gidado smiled back at me. Then he spoke to Batejo, who laughed.

"What did he say?" I demanded.

"He likes your sunglasses."

"Oh yeah, he wants them?"

Batejo spoke to him and Gidado nodded vigo-rously.

As I handed over my sunglasses to Gidado, I muttered the legal phrase *quid pro quo*, taking another lustful look at Batejo and silently promising myself to strive might and main to possess the beautiful young maiden in marriage before Gidado could get three more cows. To my dismay, I found myself secretly wishing that Gidado would not be able to get the remaining three cows. Honourable Baba Muhammed could never divine my intentions when, departing Nabordo, I asked him how much a cow cost.

"Between forty and fifty thousand naira," he replied. "But why do you ask?"

I did not reply. I was lost in thought; eight cows, costing approximately four hundred thousand naira, and Batejo would be mine!

# CHAPTER 15

The premises of the National Assembly had two gates, back and front. If I was early, as I usually was, I drove in through the front gate. But on those days when I was late, I did not use the front gate, as traffic would build up and the cars of incoming legislators, aides, visitors and civil servants would have to move at a painful crawl. Mercifully, the back entrance was reserved for legislators and was hardly ever congested. This day I acknowledged the policemen's salutes, noting with regret that I was already an hour behind the stipulated time for the commencement of plenary sessions.

I had been away from Abuja the whole of the previous week, working hard on my Conflict Resolution Bill, and was now in the dark concerning political moves and manoeuvres in the city. This made me uncomfortable, even tense. Twenty-four hours is enough time for a conspiracy to be brewed, nurtured and concluded. I noticed the outside broadcasting vans of two major national television stations in front of the White House. Obviously, something big was happening today. I parked and hurried to the legislative chamber. It was packed. Even the usually empty seats of often absent Honourable Members, whom we referred to jokingly as 'foreign based members', were occupied. My mailbox was bulging with letters, packages and huge envelopes.

I trod gingerly down the green-carpeted aisle, bowed and quietly took my seat.

The Speaker was making a speech.

Elizabeth smiled at me, whispering," You rascal, where have you been?"

I briefed her about my trip to the United Kingdom and my journey to Fulani communities to prepare a Bill.

"Don't tell me you have started running after Fulani skirts! Prepare your buttocks very well for you have to go through a flogging ceremony before you can marry any of them and I know you are too cowardly for that."

We laughed. I redirected my attention to the Speaker.

"Honourable Members," he was saying," the only order of the day is a Bill for an Act to Amend the Constitution of the Federal Republic of Nigeria (Hb 248-), Second Reading."

My surprise was complete. When did it all start?

"Lizzy," I said, "what's going on? Are we amending the Constitution?"

"Ha, ha, but of course. Are you kidding or what, Samuel? You and the Speaker are close pals. You should have known about this."

"Yes, we're close," I replied.

"And he did not bother to tell you that Chief Oneya wants one more term via a constitutional amendment?"

"What!" I exclaimed. "Lizzy you don't mean it. What kind of joke …"

The Chief Whip's voice rang out "Order, order."

I had raised my voice without knowing it.

The Speaker was still talking. "Dear colleagues, I consider it pertinent that prior to the commencement of debate on the general principles of the Constitution of the Federal Republic of Nigeria Amendment Bill, I address you on the subject. This Bill marks once again a defining moment in our march towards nationhood, as we shall through it pursue with utmost zeal, the forces of integration such that the Nigeria of our dreams will become a reality in our time. I invite your attention to Section 9 of our Constitution, subsections (1), (2), (3) and (4) with regard to the mode of altering any of its provisions. This is the course we are embarking on now.

"We should, in the course of our debate, assure all Nigerians, of whatever region or religion, that this exercise is not programmed to benefit anyone personally. It is not planned to rebound to the advantage of any person or class of persons; it is rather meant to be an impartial and patriotic undertaking, an exercise of responsibility, constitutionally vested in us, for the collective good of all Nigerians."

Elizabeth moved closer, nudged me and whispered, "A big fat lie! We know where this is coming from and we shall fight it to the end."

The Speaker continued, "We shall pursue the process of amendment in accordance with the guide contained in Section 9 of the Constitution, but will be cautious in expanding it. As the presiding officer of this House, I will like to assure you, Honourable Members, and the generality of the citizens of this great country that I will in no way deviate from the provisions of the Constitution but rather will sustain its inviolability and preserve its sanctity."

Shaking my head, I turned to Lizzy, "But I still can't believe prolonging the President's tenure is part of the Bill. Ah, ah, I thought your party had made up its mind that it is the turn of the North to produce the next President? This dirty game they call politics ..."

"Have you not checked your mail, Sam? The yellow document will give you the complete works, tell the entire story."

True enough, in the heap of my mail was a bound yellow document. I flipped through it. Its title was clear enough; "Why Tenure Prolongation is Good for Nigeria."

At that point, applause from a section of the chamber brought my attention back to the Speaker: "I urge my colleagues to stick to the general principles of the debate, to be issue-oriented, to accommodate every opinion, however novel or radical it may be, believing and knowing that at the end of it all, the minority will have their say, the majority their way, in this country where democracy is our mainstay."

A loud murmur of disapproval swept through a section of the chamber.

The Chief Whip cried," Order!"

"There will be another fire in this House very soon and not all the slush money from the Presidency will put it out," said a Member from Jigawa State sitting behind me.

The Speaker was not yet done with his speech. "I will not tolerate any attempt to muzzle any Member who has been given leave to speak on any issue, as that will be derogating from the right of such a Member. We have to constantly remind ourselves that the rule of law must be observed, but that its observance must be seen to be adhered to in all our actions. Politics, I submit, is a realistic good not a necessary evil. Long live the Federal Republic of Nigeria."

As the Speaker stopped speaking, one section of the chamber applauded while another hissed. I made up my mind to see the Speaker after the sitting. Unfortunately, I met a crowd at his office. A group from the International Red Cross was seeking audience with him, his Chief of Staff told me. He was also going to honour three other groups before rushing off to Kaduna to open a trade fair. After that, the Chief of Staff continued, he would jet down to Lagos to preside as special guest of honour at a book launch in honour of the Chief Justice of the Federation. I decided to see the House Leader instead, but the middle-aged former university lecturer stonewalled me. "Why don't you go and study the Bill first before running loose with your comments?" he asked.

Luckily, I met the Deputy Speaker as he was settling down to lunch in his office. He gave me a rundown. "Samuel, I will not lie to you: the Bill seeks an overall amendment, yes, but for us one, two, three, four areas are central. Issue number one is the creation of states; issue number two is the funding of the National Assembly; issue number three is the tenure prolongation and …"

"Tenure prolongation for whom?" I cut in.

"For the President and by extension the current political office-holders."

"But we cannot possibly extend the tenure of the President," I stated, "when everyone knows it is the turn of the North to provide the next President."

"Honourable Samuel, politics is not arithmetic. One plus one may not always equal two. In this country clean politics is a loser's game. How do you want to survive? To be a good politician you must think of your survival, of yourself first. How much did you spend to win your seat? Election expenses will continue to rise. If you come across an opportunity to return to your seat at little cost, will you not jump at it? Sam, answer me now."

I stroked my chin. "DS, you don't understand. The South West can afford to be complacent. It is our turn. The North will set the country on fire if we are cheated. We must produce the next President, or else."

The Deputy Speaker roared with laughter. "My dear Samuel, you have a long way to go in politics. Don't let me let the cat out of the bag but something is coming, heavy, like a big fat cow, something so tempting you will not be able to resist supporting the Bill."

I got up to go. At the door, I said, "DS, I beg to differ. It is painful that just a few weeks ago you and I were on the same side fighting a common cause as worthy comrades. Now we are on different sides. Let me tell you point blank: the cause you are promoting is a lost one, a hopelessly lost one."

The Deputy Speaker looked up from the meal set before him. "Hon. Samuel, that is the way of politics. Don't worry. As the saying goes, there are no permanent friends in politics, only permanent interests. Let me assure you that the minute you change your mind you are welcome to our group."

\* \* \*

Later that day I found myself in a group of like-minded legislators opposed to certain clauses in the Consti-tutional Amendment Bill. Our meeting was in the Conference Hall of the Hotel Royale at Wuse Zone 5. As the legislators followed each other into the expansive hall, I recalled what the Deputy Speaker had said about permanent interest in politics. All too true.

We were an admixture of colleagues from the Speaker's group and erstwhile adversaries from Wenike's group. Lizzy was one of us. Wenike and Honourable Lasisi were absent; they were now with the Deputy Speaker. Hitherto unknown faces were present: Hon. Yellow of Oyo State, Delta's Angel Marlabo, Hon. Olympus from Plateau State and Hon. Chike from Imo State. There was also Hon. 'Socrates', so nicknamed on account of his balding head, bushy beard and high cerebral output. In all, we were twenty-five.

In short order, we had made Hon. Abdul Kalkulus, a radical and articulate Honourable Member from Kastina our leader. I expressed my anxiety about how few we were.

"Revolutions," Hon. Kalkulus reassured me, "do not start with a crowd. All you need to change the world is a small group, dedicated, loyal and focused on big things."

Hon. Yellow then expressed his fear that we might not be able to stop the house from getting the required two-thirds majority necessary to pass the controversial Bill in view of the time constraints. He added that lots of money had been earmarked by the Presidency as a sweetener for legislators who agreed to push the Bill. "My fear" he said, "is that once this money comes, many of our members will capitulate."

We conferred: assignments were given out to Members. We gave Hon. Chike, a well-known firebrand lawyer from Imo, the task of reviewing the bill in liaison with Hon. Abel Baba, a young human rights lawyer from Edo State. Hon. Socrates volunteered to do internet research on the history of tenure prolongations.

Dishing out instructions, Hon. Kalkulus called on us all to be ready to make sacrifices when called upon in the onerous task ahead. He said, "Your other colleagues will be offered mouthwatering amounts of money to secure the passage of the Bill. In God's name, don't let that move you. Remain unshaken. The honourable verdict of history awaits you. What you are doing is writing your name in gold. And this is not the time for frivolities such as taking your spouse and children to dinners. It is time for hard work and sacrifice." He asked Yellow, Olympus and me to stay back for a very important assignment since, as he put it, "You don't have any wife to hang on to your coat-tails. You can stay on for as long as I wish."

## CHAPTER

# 16

As a pale reluctant light seeped through the window and started to unwrap itself before her eyes, the lady crept out of the bed as quietly as she could. But she was not quiet enough; the Deputy Speaker stirred. "I've got to go," she said in an urgent whisper.

"What?" he croaked. You won't stay for breakfast? It's just seven."

"No, I must go," she repeated.

"Oh, honey-pie. What's the hurry?"

"Pressing problems," she said stroking his chin tenderly.

"When will I see you again?"

"You want to? …it depends …"

He stretched beneath the bed sheets. "I must see you again." He was completely tension-free; his whole face and body was a study in contentment. Yet he wanted more of the girl. His wife and children were back home in Calabar. He had met the girl a few days ago at the White House and it had meant hours and hours of blissful comfort.

"Do you really want to see me again?" the girl asked.

The Deputy House Leader nodded and asked for her number.

"No, I'll call you," she said.

"What, are you playing hard to get? Don't forget that I

paid you well and always will."

"No, it's not that. My jealous boyfriend never allows me to take phone calls at home."

He snatched his bedside pad, scribbled a number quickly and handed it to her. "By the way, what is your name?"

"Angelina."

As Angelina left the Deputy Leader's residence in the legislators' quarters, a taxi with the colours of the Abuja Leasing Company was waiting for her at the corner leading to the Senate President's house. In the taxi, she brought out her mobile phone, tapped out the numbers rapidly and made a call. Gleefully and quietly she said, "Sir, it's done. I have all the information you want. Where do we meet?"

The taxi sped and eventually came to a halt an hour later in front of a grey duplex building in the highbrow Abuja area of Maitama. As instructed, she handed over two tapes and the memory stick from a digital camera to a secretary waiting for her in the office. In return, she collected a fat white envelope. She split the envelope, thumbed the freshly-minted naira notes rapidly, uttered a curt 'Thank you' and disappeared into the bowels of the city.

\* \* \*

It took me days of gruelling effort to track the Speaker down. Finally, I was told on the third day at his official residence that he had not yet come down from his first-floor bedroom. I waited with a few other visitors and contractors for close to an hour before the tall spare figure descended the stairs. His eyes were a little bloodshot; his movements were slow; he dragged his feet. He brightened up, sighting me. "Hello Samuel, I am sorry I have not had time to see you. Please come over, let's have breakfast."

As we tackled the *koko* and *kose*, I gave the Speaker an update on my activities. "I came to thank you about my Bill. It has passed the second reading and has been committed to the House

Committee on Conflict Resolution."

"Great! This is what I have always said. This Bill will make history! Can you count the number of people waiting for it to pass? The Bill will solve many problems within and outside the country once it is passed," the Speaker observed.

"Thank you, Sir. We shall need your assistance on the public hearing which I want to take place as soon as possible."

"Oh, Sam, you are always welcome. What is your budget for that?"

"Five million naira, Sir."

"Make it seven. Invite as many Fulanis as possible. This will be the first time I have brought my kinsmen to Abuja. I will suggest some names to you. I am building up my political base, you know," he said, winking.

"That I will do, Sir."

"One more point. You will need to involve the Committee on Agriculture because we are trying to see how we can give the Fulani designated land for grazing. Get in touch with Hon. Hassan Lawal, the Chairman of the Agric. Committee."

The talk about my Bill over, the Speaker went straight to the point. Looking me intently in the eyes and dropping his cutlery at the same time, he said, "Hon. Samuel, you are being difficult."

I smiled warmly and stopped eating.

"Unnecessarily difficult, Sam. I am not happy with what I'm hearing about you and the Constitutional Review Bill. Ah, ah, Sam, did I not confide in you about Chief's special interest in the Bill? The President means well. Now, as the Tenure Prolongation Bill sails through, it's honey for us all. We shall all smile. Who does not know it costs a fortune to run around campaigning these days? Now, you won't have to run around. Imagine, Sam, you just sit in your armchair with an automatic ticket falling into your lap. Or you are thinking of returning to your law practice? There's more money in politics. My advice is not to leave this place."

"Mr. Speaker, do you want me to deceive you or to tell you the truth?"

"Sam, come straight to the point today. There is no truth in politics, only compromises. The truth we have forgotten."

I continued defiantly, "The truth, Mr. Speaker, is that it is the turn of the North. Do we want the country on fire? What will our people say when they hear you have given their right on a platter of friendship to a President who does not really like you and but for God's mercies would have thrown you off the Speaker's chair?"

The Speaker stared hard at me and said nothing. He poured himself another cup of tea and quietly slowly added first one and then a second drop of honey to the cup; he stirred the mixture, moving the spoon as if it had suddenly turned heavy. He took a sip.

"Samuel, are you really a politician? Have you forgotten the saying, No permanent friends, only permanent interests? Let me tell you, it is a truism. That is one. The President was against me in the past, now he is for me. Two, the North. The people of the North? They are an amorphous sociological mass, not a political entity. The people. Which people? Our hungry passive constituents? What do they care about politics? The hungry masses will go for anything. At any rate, my own take ... what is at stake for us is to give the President our support. Life is a risk. And this is a good risk. If the plan succeeds, all well and good. If it doesn't, we have nothing to lose. You and I, Sam, all of us would at least have gained some money."

I sipped some tea. How could I mollify him, I wondered. After a while, I spoke. "I agree, Mr. Speaker. Still, you need to maintain an appearance of neutrality in this matter. Consider, if the President's bid, which you are supporting, fails in the end, your political career will be at grave risk. Let the Deputy Speaker and Deputy Leader be the aggressive activists. Let them handle it while you take a back seat."

Wale Okediran

\* \* \*

Deliberately, I allowed my intense emotions on the Tenure Prolongation Bill to cool off. The Conflict Resolution Bill and Batejo were now centre-stage in my mind. Returning to Nabordo the following week, principally to put finishing touches to preparations for the public hearing, was paramount. I took out the file, read the title for the umpteenth time – A Bill For An Act To Establish A Commission For Pastoralists and Agriculturalists in the Federal Republic of Nigeria – and smiled. I packed Batejo's package-books and other gifts with red as the colour motif. How would I connect with the girl without drawing undue attention to myself?

Hon. Baba Muhammed, in whom I had confided regarding my interest in the girl, advised me to plan my trip for a market day. He said, "In the bubbles and buzz of a market day you can see her without attracting undue attention."

It was midday. The market was full. The crowd milled all over the settlement of Nabordo. Gaily dressed boys and girls were everywhere, showing off their headscarves, sunglasses, radios and in some cases new handsets. They lined up at a nearby photo studio for their pictures to be taken. They struck poses, adjusting their earrings and lipsticks. The photographer, a young Ibo man, entered their names in a notebook since many of them were going to pick up and pay for their pictures on the next market day.

I roamed around wondering if this or that item would catch my eye. The market was well-organised; each ware had its own section. At the hardware section, young men bought and sharpened cutlasses. Some of them fixed new leather handles on their cutlasses. In another section of the market, a local medicine man held court. Cheerfully, he broadcast the power of his array of traditional medicinal plants, powders and bottled fluids. He boasted that he could cure all illness and diseases. He ran off a long list of afflictions including stomach ache, coughs, fever and snake bite. On sighting me, he stroked his beard furiously, roared with laughter and, with frequent use of an obscene gesture, sought to harangue me into purchasing an aphrodisiac guaranteed to establish my prowess with any woman, young or old, wife or paramour.

Suddenly feeling hungry and following my nose, I found the cooked-food section. The tantalizing aroma was unmistakable. In a corner of the market, women were sweating over sizzling pots of fried yam, yam pottage, rice and beans. For me, the most fascinating part of the market was the cattle section. Herds in hired trucks were sold to eager buyers at an average price of forty thousand naira. Surveying the cattle, I reminded myself of the eight Batejo cows. Hawkers called out their goods stridently. Itinerant CD and DVD vendors had their players blaring out music at full volume. Completing the cacophony were the loudspeakers of the itinerant medicine sellers pushing their remedies and potions in wheelbarrows.

Hanging permanently in the air in conflict with each other were the odour of sweat and cow dung and the appetizing aroma of food.

\* \* \*

I met the elders of Nabordo in the Sarkin Fulani cattle shed. I did not want the Sarkin to close shop for the meeting so we agreed that the brief meeting would be held amidst the hustle and bustle of buying and selling in the market. As she had the minutes of our last meeting with her, Batejo was sent for. My happiness knew no bounds at her sight as I found myself smiling broadly. We needed to check the records to confirm the names of those coming for the public hearing. Ardor welled up in my heart again as I glimpsed Batejo's aquiline nose and fair features afresh. An irresistible wave of longing swept over me. I must marry this girl, I said in my heart, and in the next few months. She greeted with impressive warmth.

The meeting over, I told her to go ahead and wait for me at the photographer's shop where I promised to see her on the way back to Abuja. Later, there, I handed her package over to her. She thanked me happily for the books and the tiny dainty red bag. She peered inside the bag. "What's inside?" she asked gaily.

"A mobile phone and a packet of chocolates." She beamed her delight and thanks.

"Do you know how to use the phone?" I asked.

She shook her head.

I showed her how to dial and send text messages. She frowned in concentration and I encouraged her, telling her she could not of course learn all the details at once.

"Read the phone manual. Read it very well. And if nothing else, remember my phone number. It's already there, stored for you. What should I bring for you next time, red girl?"

She smiled demurely, showing small even white teeth. "This is enough for now. Do you like local cheese? I will ask my mother to pack a load for you sir, against … will you come on the next market day?"

I ignored everything and asked as if it was important, "Where is Gidado?"

"Oh, he has …" she began, tucking away the gifts into her handbag, "he is gone with his cattle. He won't be around for at least three days."

"Has he brought any more cows?" I asked.

She laughed and shook her head.

"Suppose," I asked, pausing and gazing at the sky as if at a flying plane," Suppose I bring eight cows to your father, will you marry me?"

She covered her face with her hands, laughing. "I don't know what my parents will say," she said moments later.

I told her I held her in genuine affection and wondered if she would drop everything and follow me as my wife to go and live in Abuja. "Abuja," I assured her," is a city full of books. You will read to your heart's content, watch television and learn about other countries."

She gazed at me in wonder and started laughing again.

"Have you been to Abuja before?" I asked.

"No, but I have an elder sister who lives there."

"And what did she tell you about Abuja?"

She answered, "She said it is a nice civilised city… *ehn, ehn*, they say in Abuja the bus conductors wear neckties to work and many taxi drivers have Master's degrees …"

"By my fine whiskers, who has been laying it on thick for you?" I exclaimed.

"What does 'laying it on thick' mean, please?"

"Lying, fibbing, exaggerating," I said.

"No, not my sister – the photographer opposite," she said.

"Oh, well, it's not it. Abuja is OK, but not that sophisticated. We are still in good old Africa. Will you visit your sister one of these days, so that I can take you round Abuja?"

She nodded vigorously and gave me another hearty smile.

Just then, two of her friends summoned her to come over to take photographs. She hesitated then shook her head.

"Go," I admonished. "Here, take some money for a personal photograph which you must give me."

She passed the money and the gifts to her friends who all said "*Mun gode, Min yatti*" thanking me in Hausa and Fulfude on behalf and in support of Batejo.

Back from the photographer, I asked Batejo to see me off to my car. She declined. "Tongues will wag and Gidado will be mad."

"But you are not yet married. So you can't talk to other men, only Gidado?"

She laughed again, shaking her head.

"I would like to see you again. On the next market day," I said.

She gave no reply. I repeated my request.

She laughed and whispered a faint "Yes".

"Don't bother about local cheese, my sweet red girl. But I will bring you more books and chocolates. Before then, I will phone you. Tell your parents you are helping government with your literacy skills. And that government has been kind and sweet and loving enough to give you a phone and other things. One more thing," I said and called her line. The ringing of the phone startled her. I showed her how to receive the call and then taught her how to call me back.

"If your parents or Gidado ask you how you came about the phone, just tell them its part of the things the government gave you to assist in your new job … *kin gane?*"

She nodded.

As I bade her farewell, she waved gaily to me. In the three hours it took me to drive back to Abuja, I called my sweet red girl more than ten times. Deep within me, I had the sweet feeling she would be mine. Eventually.

# CHAPTER 17

Early one morning, I got a phone call from the Principal Secretary to the President, inviting me to a breakfast meeting in the Presidential villa, popularly called Aso Rock by most Nigerians. Aso Rock, an expansive and palatial structure, is both residence and office to Nigeria's Head of State. With the rumour of the prolongation plan thick in the air like harmattan in January, it was obvious that the breakfast meeting would be an extraordinary gathering convened for an extraordinary purpose. All week, Presidential aides and party chieftains had vetted the list of those to be invited to the meeting. For one reason or another, the privilege of being part of the extraordinary group had been extended to me.

Aso Rock has never failed to impress me with its grandeur. Enclosed amidst an aggregation of towering rocks intricately set in place by Mother Nature, hedged round by a man-made canal and shielded from easy view by big trees and tall shrubbery, the villa had obviously been designed by an architect with his mind set on maximum security. America has its grand White House, well over a century and a half old; India has its one-thousand-room Rasthrapathi Bhaur, the awesome abode of its President in New Delhi; and Britain has its functional Number 10 Downing Street; but Nigeria can also be proud of its Aso Rock with its deceptively simple yet futuristic aesthetics. The enchanting greenery, the immaculate manicured lawns and the soothing palms that yield in the gentle wriggle to the rhythm of the daylight breeze together with all-white coating of the structures makes for a sprawling and picturesque villa.

After the usual security checks and long waits for accreditation, we were finally ushered in. As usual, we had to pass through several gates and at each gate we had to go through accreditation. While waiting in the Council Chambers alongside other guests for the President's arrival, my mind drifted to former occupants of the villa; the consecutive trio of ruling Generals: the crafty Ibrahim Babangida, the psycopathic Sanni Abacha and the quickly efficient Abdulsalam Abubakar, a wealthy man today. Their aides also came to mind: Ahaji Ismail Gwarzo, Brigadier-General Sabo Mohammed, Major Hamza Al-Mustapha, Sergeant Barnabas Msheila and their kind who once held court in the place.

Looking across the courtyard, I recalled how Abacha and his infamous son Mohammed allegedly tortured the so-called suspects of the phantom coup he fabricated. One of the victims said they were stripped naked in the open courtyard and icy water was poured on them in the chilly harmattan of January, followed by lashes of a horsewhip before they were eventually thrown into filthy dungeons. In my imagination I saw Babangida holding court, as verily he did, and receiving delegation after delegation of eminent Nigerians who had come to see him on the issue of the annulled national June 12 elections. It was said that the foxy Head of State had shown his visitors documents which is said formed the basis of his refusal to allow Bashorun MKO Abiola, the putative winner of the election, his rightful position.

I was still lost in thought amid the chatter and banter, the laughing and backslapping of the other guests when an exclusive door opened and a Presidential aide announced the arrival of Mr. President accompanied by the Vice President. He looked completely different from the cartoon caricature of a sleepy-eyed and gaunt-looking man with oversized ear lobes sticking out like a rabbit's. President Oneya appeared smart, even hand-some, that is if you ignored the large dark mole on the tip of his nose.

In the first few minutes of the meeting, the President cracked jokes, gently accusing the Speaker of having forgotten him after he had helped him regain his seat. I recalled my previous encounters with the President. In all four of them, I have found him eager to talk, down-to-earth and, to say the least, quick-witted. And when you thought about his background as a banker-turned-politician, now the leader of the world's most populous black nation, you would expect him to be shrewd and crafty and, when necessary, ruthless.

After the small talk, we settled down to breakfast. It was a gathering of those that mattered in the quest for tenure prolongation. Seated next to the President was Vice President Davou Pam, tucking expressionlessly into his *Koko* and *Kose* with the deft air of an artisan plastering a freshly-made wall. At the far end of the table, discreetly checking the mobile phone that he had smuggled into the meeting against standard regulations, was Senator Smollet. The Speaker and his Vice whispered to each other as they shovelled away forkfuls of rice and beans.

The rest of us were scattered all over the spacious dining hall as waiters moved around taking and answering orders. Sitting next to me was a Member from Abia State. He seemed to be impatient as he cast furtive glances at his wristwatch. "Do you know when the President will speak?" he asked me.

"I believe that it will have to be after we have eaten."

Then, leaning close to me, he whispered, "Are we collecting the stuff today? You know what I mean?" he said, rubbing the tips of the fingers of his right hand in a gesture of counting wads of currency.

I couldn't resist laughing. But I then told him I wasn't aware of money being shared that day. While the breakfast remnants and the plates and cutlery were being carted away, the President struck his spoon against a tumbler to attract attention. He thanked us for honouring his invitation, congratulated all of us on the beautiful job we had been doing in moving the nation forward and admonished us to work harder as more work still needed to be done. He said, "My fellow countrymen, one of these tasks is in the area of Constitution review. As you all know, the 1999 Constitution is an imperfect document. Therefore I want you all to work earnestly towards correcting its gross errors.

"There are over a hundred amendments in the Bill but regrettably the focus of most people is exclusively on the tenure prolongation clause. As stakeholders in the current democratic exercise, it is vital that we put aside sentiments, eschew vile talk and rumour mongering and continue the noble task of nation-building. You must understand the need for consolidation since frequent changes of government tend to erode the gains of democracy. All over Africa, our leaders are very much aware of the urgent need for continuity. This is why, in Uganda and Algeria, Presidents Yoweri Museveni and Abdelaziz Bouteflica respectively were able to get their third-term tenure. In nearby Niger, the President is currently organising mass rallies in all the provinces of the country to support the Constitutional change which will give him his third term in office. We therefore need to be careful as we tackle the Constitutional Review Project." As he spoke, his professional eyes did not betray a hint of his own views on the matter. "As the father of the nation, my duty is to guide you on the right path. Whatever may be your final decision about tenure prolongation, I sincerely pray that it will be a decision that will take the country to greater heights, peace and progress."

As the President continued his speech, an air of gloom and uncertainty filled the air. While the supporters of the President's tenure prolongation scheme expected him to be more forthcoming in his request, his opponents were befuddled at what they termed the President's double talk. A few minutes later, the President finished his speech. We then clapped, more out of courtesy than appreciation. Thereafter some guests who had been notified earlier were asked to wait to see the President in two separate rooms.

The Member from Abia State who sat next to me must have been one of those who were slated to see the President, as he looked quite bright and cheerful once the meeting came to an end. His clapping was enthusiastic. "Isn't that beautiful?" he asked me. "One of the best speeches I've ever heard," he purred before moving to the adjoining meeting room with others. I was still wondering what the import of the whole meeting was when a presidential aide summoned me. The President was waiting for me as I entered what appeared to be an office. Seated at his right was the Vice President with his expressionless face. A native of Jos, the reverend gentleman was reputed to be the spearhead of the tenure prolongation bid, not because he believed in it but because he believed in peace. He went along with the tide so as not to rock the boat. He coveted peace of mind above all else. At sixty-five, he was five years older than the President and wanted no hassles from the younger man. He had confided in some journalists that his modest ambition was just four more years in government so that he could celebrate his seventieth birthday in peace surrounded by his children and grandchildren.

"Honourable Samuel," the President said, shaking my hand. "I am sure you have met the Vice President. VP, you surely remember this Honourable Member. We saw him on TV during the demonstration by the students and workers at the National Assembly. A very energetic and promising young man, I must say."

I smiled. "I am still learning the ropes, Mr. President." I said, hoping that I was not being set up for something unwholesome.

"Please sit down, Samuel," the President said waving me to a seat. "I called you to sound you out. Em … em. What do you think of my speech?"

"Your speech, Mr. President, well, …em …em … I found it okay, balanced," I said, a little untruthfully. Actually, what I meant to say was that it was an uncomfortable and disturbing speech but I chose to be polite and hence insincere.

The Vice President coughed, and shifted nervously in his seat.

"Thank you, Sam, in that case, we are on the same footing. You see, I have followed your progress since you came to the National Assembly. You are, no doubt, a brilliant young man, the type that can move this great country forward. As you very well know, governance is a slow process. It takes a while to get anything out of the process and for that reason, frequent changes in government does not augur well for continuity. As a well-educated man I am sure you are conversant with political history. You and I know that too-frequent changes of government can be disruptive to good governance. It takes most governments in developing countries some four years to find their feet. These four years are not a waste; they are just long enough for a regime to struggle through before it can manifest positive signs of progress.

"The fact that we are authentic democrats, self-declared observers of the rule of law, due process and constitutional democracy does not mean we should not think of the overall benefit to the nation of our actions. We must avoid blind servitude to the constitution. To adapt a biblical phrase, 'Man is not made for the constitution but the constitution is made for man.'"

The Vice President coughed again. I looked up to catch a faint bemused smile on his placid face.

The President took a sip from a glass of water by his side. "The constitution, I repeat, is a guide not a manacle, a beacon not a chain. Samuel, you will remember Harold Macmillan, the British Prime Minister who bent to the wind of political opinion and suffered the whirlwind of public disapproval. Macmillan destroyed his own government by bowing to pressure for a change – he sacked a third of his own cabinet, a massacre dubbed the Night of the Long Knives! The bitter consequence: Macmillan himself was out of office the following year. That is a mistake that I, Oneya, am not anxious to repeat. My dear Sam, I am thinking of a controlled and mature approach. I am in fact not suggesting anything; all I am trying to do is guide you. Guided democracy it is called and I need your help."

Now that the President had become direct and open, I decided to be sincere. "If your direction and vision are thus inclined, Mr. President," I said, "one has to state unambiguously that the idea of tenure prolongation is at worst controversial and at best a non-starter. I am being sincere, Sir; for one thing, many House Members will be uncomfortable with their governors continuing in office. But more importantly, the North believes it's their turn at Aso Rock …"

"In that case," the President broke in, "we can extend the tenure prolongation idea to the legislature. *Em … em …* VP, what do you think?"

The Vice-President coughed, shifted nervously in his seat and nodded. "I agree with his Excellency and …"

The President broke in again. "Because, Samuel, as you very well know, we are not doing anything new. Tenure prolongation has been practised worldwide for ages by democracies like Indonesia and Malaysia, not to mention several African countries such as Zimbabwe, Uganda, Cameroun and Algeria, just to mention a few. Even the US Congress once decided to extend the tenure of George Washington. So, my dear Samuel, what do you now think?" The President spoke as one determined to ride roughshod over any opposition. His eyes became fixed and his voice took on a rapid agitated tone. I came to realize that power is a drug; some men are drawn to it like moth to a candle. This man was one of those souls drawn towards it, as to a magnet, notwithstanding the dangers. He was fully charged, ready to risk his life, career and reputation for the sake of power.

I began my answer. "You Excellency, apart from Malaysia, the other examples of tenure prolongation experiments mostly ended badly. My feeling is that here in this great country the idea may not fly. In fact, it may truncate our democracy. Let us not lose to it all the goodwill we have amassed over the years."

The Vice-President coughed again. That was about it. I knew the meeting was over. As the President saw me to the door, I could see in the Vice President's eyes a glint of satisfaction.

## CHAPTER 18

I left for Nabordo the day after my encounter with the President. Since my last visit to the *riga* two weeks earlier, Batejo and I had been in constant touch by phone. It was a bittersweet situation. While we were always happy to chat, the report from Batejo that Gidado was aware of my overtures to her disturbed me greatly and saddened Batejo herself intensely.

"He said you gave me the phone so as to woo me. He has tried to seize the phone. I hid it in my brassière, and it's on silent mode at all times now," she said.

Gidado, she told me, had warned her not to see me again but she told him the preparations for the forthcoming public hearing were unavoidable. For this little window of opportunity I was quite glad. I asked her, "Does that mean you won't see me again once the public hearing is over?"

"It will be difficult, but you know what to do if you want to see me after that. The ball is in your court."

I knew what she meant. It was neither the issue of the cows nor even the matter of her betrothal to Gidado. Getting eight dowry cows was not the problem and the betrothal to Gidado could be reversed. The major obstacle, "the ball in my court" in finally getting the hand of Batejo in marriage was the demand that I should convert to Islam. My family antecedents were deeply Christian and the Bakura clan would be all aflame in dissent and denial if I reneged on the faith for a bride and marriage. For me, Batejo was worth any sacrifice; an innocent, unspoiled girl head-over-heels in love with me, wise beyond her years and with a thirst for education. Deep inside me, I knew conversion to Islam was a step I would joyfully take to have Batejo's hand in marriage.

    I reached Narbodo at noon and spent the next two hours putting finishing touches to matters in a meeting with the elders concerning the public hearing. As usual, Batejo was at the meeting. The market was our rendez-vous and I asked her to go there ahead of me. I had brought from Abuja not just new books but a small diamond ring to mark 'our engagement'. I had discovered a secluded part of the market and there I planned to give her the ring. We sat on a tree trunk shielded by wild shrubbery. I tried kissing her, but the girl would have none of it.

    "It's against our tradition," she said.

    Nevertheless, she was in high spirits. She was eager to come to Abuja for the public hearing. "I have not been to Abuja before, although as you know I have heard good stories about it," she said. When I told her that the public hearing was coming up in two weeks' time, she became worried. "That means you have to move fast if you want my hand in marriage. After the public hearing I will not have any excuse to see you again."

    I told her not to worry, that I was set to come over with the dowry cows and talk with her parents.

    "What about the conversion?" she asked. "That must come before any other thing."

    "Yes. But what is the procedure? Am I expected to do it publicly or privately?"

    "You can do it quietly. You will approach an Imam with one or two friends of yours. You will need to accept that Allah is only one and that he does not have a son or daughter and that Mohammed is his last messenger."

    I laughed. "But by my wig and gown we have an elementary contradiction here. We Christians believe that Jesus Christ is the Son of God."

Batejo, gently fiddling with my handset, also laughed. "You say you love me. Make the sacrifice, forget the differences between the two religions and cross over to mine," she said, with smiling eyes and a tender touch to my shoulder.

"How long does conversion take?"

"Very short, about the duration of marriage vows. Ten, fifteen minutes, I think."

"What about my name? Can I still keep it or are you …"

"Lawyer Bature, I will change my surname for yours. But to convince people about your conversion you may rename yourself Ishmael."

"I prefer Dahud or Mahmud."

Ah!" she chuckled," I like Mahmud; that is my grandfather's name. It means someone who has been praised by God Himself."

"Really? After that, what's next?"

"That's all. You will learn our prayer verses, join a nearby mosque, pray five times a day and fast in the month of Ramadan."

"After that what's next is I, lawyer Mahmud Bature do thee Batejo wed …"

"*Insh' Allah*," she said, her eyes heavenwards, her hands outspread in the mode of Islamic prayer.

"Only one thing remains, my beauty and my dear: the Gidado issue."

"Gidado?" Batejo sighed. In a low tone she said," My parents will know how to handle that."

"Have you told them?"

"Told them what?"

"That I want to marry you."

She laughed. "Have you told me you want to marry me?"

Then I remembered. In a flash I brought out the shiny white case from a pocket of my caftan, plucked the ring out of it, knelt down in front of my loving and lovely Batejo, took her left hand and slipped the ring onto her third finger, crooning, "Batejo, will you marry me?"

No answer came. Two large tear drops emerged from her unblemished face as she also dropped on her knees and clung to me in ecstasy. We remained in an embrace for long moments, her face a picture of pure bliss and my body in a fever of electric excitement.

"I have to go. I don't want to be seen with you alone until you've seen my parents," she whispered in my ear, daintily, teasingly biting it. We hastily arranged our next visit. She slipped off back to the market through the footpath.

I straightened up, wiped the sand off my trousers and made for the main road where I had parked my car. Mightily pleased with the day's developments I began to whistle a love song. Suddenly the low shrill of a real whistle broke into the stillness of the afternoon. Two shrill whistles answered. Turning back, my eyes lit upon two Fulani boys approaching me nonchalantly. They were going to the market, I thought, or searching for lost cows. The whistle reminded me of my days as a university athlete and sportsman, running the four hundred metres and captaining the soccer team. I resumed whistling the love song. Then it happened. The boys broke into a sudden run and were upon me in a trice with their *sandas* striking me on my head, shoulders, back and legs. I put up a stern fight, warding off the first blows from my youthful and wiry attackers. Because they were smaller in stature, I even succeeded in hurling one of them into the other, causing them to stumble and gaining time to run down the bushy footpath. They, however, recovered quickly and, not being hobbled like me by an elegant but heavy-on-the-body dress, they soon outran me and began the pummeling again.

My first thought was that they were thieves. But then I recognized my two assailants as Aliyu and Bello, Gidado's companions. I escaped from their grip again, running for dear life. They pursued me with unflinching intent, silently and angrily. As I was about to turn around the bend on the footpath leading to the road verge where my car was, they caught up with me again. "Help! Help!" I screamed, but my voice was too hoarse from the run, I thought no one heard me. Not a word came from the boys only the relentless rain of their *sandas* on my weakening body. Suddenly I saw a dagger, then two. Murder! I pleaded for mercy at the top of my voice. The daggers hit my skin. I felt my body tearing apart; travelling across my shoulders were a series of sharp pains that then leaped to my arms and then my legs. I shut my eyes in agony and opened them only to see a crimson flood of blood. Even then, they continued cutting me as I continued screaming. I was now on the dusty ground, immobilised by the blows of the *sanda* to my legs, my caftan now ripped into shreds by the vicious and multiple knife wounds. After a while, the attack stopped as my assailants now stood and watched, their dark eyes troubled, almost sorrowful as they left me to bleed to death.

\* \* \*

For weeks the tenure prolongation agenda was on the front burner. Both chambers of the National Assembly were inundated with statements and counterstatements from speeches, rallies, symposia, seminars, press briefings, radio interviews, television talk shows and pulpits. The Northern Governors Forum, a mighty pressure group in the country, summoned a meeting in Kaduna. Most of the governors were against the idea of tenure prolongation but a few supported it. One Alhaji Zango Mohammed, the spokesperson of the Forum, said, "We concede that the 1999 Constitution is not a perfect document. However, its fallibility cannot be used as an excuse for legislative tinkering and chicanery in the pursuit of a personal agenda. We unequivocally condemn in the strongest possible terms the whole idea of the ongoing constitutional amendment whose primary objective is to achieve the third-term agenda."

Among those who addressed the Northern Governors at

the meeting was a famous Senator and former Federal Minister, Senator Ogo A. Ogochukwu. He said that he and members of his group, the 2007 Movement, would stop at nothing to block the third-term project. "We shall," the Senator stated, "be victims of calamity and culprits of history if the tension precipitated by the third-term agenda sets the country on the path of self-destruction."

In an open letter to the federal legislators, a governor from one of the States in the South-East geopolitical zone, Dr Obed Luka, described the third-term idea as "a booby trap". He continued, "For me, the third-term agenda is ungodly and uncharitable. It is subversive ... but you representatives have to do something fast to counter the rumours going round that some of you have been bought over to support the agenda." A former Nigerian leader, a retired army general, spoke stridently against the third-term agenda. His was a powerful voice. President Oneya found his opposition a bitter pill to swallow. He looked the other way as his aides launched on a tirade against the retired general.

Even some people who were close to the President at one time or other communicated with Members of the National Assembly urging them not to betray their consciences or to compromise the future of the generality of Nigerians. The media attacked the third-term agenda in editorial after editorial. Cartoonists had a field day satirizing the agenda and columnists saw no merit whatsoever in it. A few pro-government news-papers wrote in support of the third-term project but their heart was not in it.

The Governors in support of the third-term agenda became President Oneya's friends and cronies while those against it became the targets of the nation's anticorruption agency. In a South-Eastern State, President Oneya sponsored hoodlums and arsonists to destabilize an anti-third-term Governor's regime. In another Middle-Belt State whose Governor was opposed to the agenda, the state lawmakers were sponsored to impeach the Governor even without the required two-thirds majority. War was also waged against the legislators. At first they were persuaded to join the third-term gravy train, they were assured that their own tenures would be elongated. They were assured of automatic re-election and zero naira campaign expenses.

However, when this approach failed, party leaders and Governors were mandated to force their hands. When, again, this plan failed, the ultimate bait of money was resorted to. This aspect of the plan was cleverly put together by government contractors in the private sector, officials of the Central Bank and Presidential aides. The money – half a million US dollars per legislator! – arrived in Abuja in green diplomatic bags on board a private airline from Lagos one April evening. At the airport to receive the consignment was the spearhead of the Presidential aides in charge of the operation, Dr Ambrose Kalu. With the help of some government officials, the money was spirited to a bank owned by one of the President's personal friends. Though the bank had closed for business that day, lawmakers were still trooping in for their share as late as midnight.

# CHAPTER 19

Attracted by my screams, Batejo shouted for her uncle, who had a cattle stall nearby. Together they found me where I lay bleeding to death. On sighting them, my assailants took to their heels, but not before they were recognized. With the aid of some other youths in the market I was wrapped in a blanket and taken to my car. Luckily, I had come with my driver and so it was easy for them to carry me in my car to the nearest hospital, a health centre about ten minutes' drive from the village. I could barely remember the trip to the centre as I had lost a lot of blood.

Batejo, who filled me in on the details of my rescue, said on the way to the hospital that she kept feeding me with some *fura da nono* from a calabash gourd. I had no recollection of this. I came to at the point when I was being moved to a stretcher. It was soaked in blood. I saw Batejo and her uncle Tatari grimace as blood continued to spurt from my head. A female nurse spoke. "He has a deep gash here," she told a male nurse. She patted my head with tissue paper to staunch the flow of blood. She continued, "The wound, I think, is quite deep and he may need a transfusion." The female nurse turned my head to one side and started to cut away some of my hair. With a blade she shaved off the remaining hair.

The male nurse prepared a tray with needles, plaster and

cotton wool. I expected some kind of anaesthetic, but there was none. The male nurse suddenly grabbed my head, put in his first stitch and drew the flesh together. My feet drummed helplessly on the couch with pain, compelling the female nurse to hold my knees together as her colleague prepared the second stitch. I watched him as he put the second stitch and my feet started to bang together again. I was expecting some words of encouragement or sympathy such as "It's all right" or "Just one more stitch", but nothing was said by the cold-hearted, cold blooded and unsmiling nurse, plying his impassive needle, remorselessly hemming my head.

Through all the six stitches of his grisly embroidery, he uttered not a single word. I wondered what kind of nurse it was that would not utter even a word to his patient. It must be, I surmised, that his ambitions were once aimed higher than working in a remote rural health center. Was he already sinking into a routine of frustration and inanition like some of those bored office clerks in the National Assembly office who usually answered one's polite greetings with melancholic frowns? Was the daily flow of split heads and bruised lips becoming too much for him to handle? Did he expect a dash for his job? Was he perhaps aware of the circumstances of the assault on me and felt that I deserved the punishment? But nothing was said, only the mechanical cold-blooded morose man plying his needle of pain, remorselessly hemming my head.

At the final stitch, it occurred to me that he had missed his time, this expressionless cold young man, distant and lost in his own world. After the torture, the female nurse let go of my knees and smiled, saying, "Thank God for small mercies." I felt one of them at least was human.

\* \* \*

It was the third day of my stay in the National Hospital, Abuja, to which I was eventually transferred. I was still groggy from the effect of a sedative when the doctor and his team came for the ward round. "How are you today, Honourable?" asked the consultant surgeon, a young man in thick glasses.

"Fine, doctor and can I go home today?" I asked. Even though I was satisfied with the attention and service of the staff of the National Hospital Abuja where I was referred to from the health centre on the Bauchi-Jos road where I was first rushed to after the assault, I was getting bored just lying down.

"Ha, ha, Honourable, try to relax. You've been with us only three days. I don't think you are missing anything staying away from the House. From the accounts in the newspapers, nothing much is happening there except ..."

"You mean the Tenure Prolongation brouhaha," I said.

"Yes ... yes."

"That's a lot, a whole lot, you know. All the more reason why I have to return to my beat, as they say."

The Consultant conferred briefly with the Registrar. The latter spoke briskly: "The wounds are mostly superficial except for a deep one on the head which had been stitched before he got here. They should all be dry in a couple of days. We can let him go home on oral antibiotics and he can come and remove the stitches on Friday."

Turning to me, the consultant said, "You are lucky, Honourable, your wounds are healing well. We shall discharge you later today. You will return on Friday to have your stitches removed."

My discharge papers were soon perfected. I had spent three days at the hospital, six days in all. The male nurse at the health centre I remember with horror. I remembered the female nurse, smiling. The two had finally decided that I did not need a blood transfusion. I had a deep head gash but the wounds on my upper and lower limbs were superficial and needed only some form of pressure dressing. I had been given intravenous fluids for rehydration and some intravenous drugs had also been administered.

Throughout my three-day stay at the health centre, Batejo

and her uncle Tatari stayed with me. Tatari proved to be one of the most compassionate human beings I have ever met. Apart from allowing Batejo to stay with me at the rural health centre he personally paid all my hospital bills, even though I kept telling him to ask my driver for the money I had inside my car. In addition, he reported the incident to the village head, who in turn reported Gidado and his friends to their parents. One thing had cast a cloud on my thoughts, but it proved to be a needless worry: although news of the assault had gone round the market and the village, no journalist, fortunately, was around to give the incident wider coverage. I found this quite a mercy. I could imagine the news headlines or worse, the feature stories complete with Batejo's photograph: *Dalliance Lands Randy Honourable in Hospital; Honourable Bature in an untidy love triangle*, and so on and so forth.

    I learnt later that while the villagers felt for Gidado on account of my affair with Batejo, they were horrified at the brutality I was exposed to. The village head reprimanded Gidado and his friends and made them refund the money spent at the health centre while insisting that they would also refund the money spent at the National Hospital in Abuja. At the health centre, Batejo and I had spoken about our future together. Having seen the nurse at work, the human female one rather than her inhuman male counterpart I was sure, she told me she would love to become a nurse. I promised to send her to a nursing school.

    Since I was now quite friendly with Tatari, I assured Batejo that regarding marriage I would seek her uncle's support in approaching her parents. I jokingly told Batejo that since I had been assaulted by Gidado's friends I would no longer need to go through the traditional Fulani marriage rite of getting flogged. "No chickening out, Sir; you were forced then but you will have to go through the ceremony willingly. You are my strong man," she said, displaying her beautiful teeth.

    Tatari, but not Batejo, accompanied me to Abuja but we

were constantly on the phone and she cried often as we said goodbye at the end of each call.

\* \* \*

The next meeting of the 2007 Movement took place at the Conference Hall of the Diamond Hotel at Asokoro in Abuja late one evening. I had missed a couple of meetings as a result of the Gidado assault, but I was pleasantly surprised to notice that the attendance had improved, in fact doubled. There were only twenty-five of us the last time I was at the meeting but our ranks had swollen to fifty. Lizzy snorted when I mentioned this to her. "What! We are much fewer. Last week, we were over a hundred."

"My, what happened?" I asked.

"What happened? Where have you been? American wonder – the money, of course. Didn't you hear about the five hundred thousand American dollars? It has blown away so many Members."

Some guests who had been invited to talk with us soon arrived. They were the ambassadors of four European countries. They outlined the dangers of the tenure prolongation plan and pledged the support of their countries to our cause. Their one demand was that we should be steadfast and unwavering in our determination. We continued our meeting after our guests had taken their leave.

Worried by the mass desertion of our camp by Members who had been subjected to heavy pressure, some Members suggested that we also look for money to retain our loyalists. The debate see-sawed until Honourable Socrates spoke with his accustomed verve, convincing us all: "I have gone through the annals of the history of politics and politicians. I have come to the conclusion that the one enduring factor in the calculus of political success is determination: determination allied with integrity and group cohesion. The moment you mix filthy lucre with political virtue you find you are in quicksands of failure. A pure vision unclouded by money politics will bring us victory, fellow patriots. Finally, if we can sustain the tempo of our campaign, extend the catchment area of our support to the media and labour without losing the backing of the diplomatic corps, our political foes will never get the golden two-thirds majority."

Hon. Ogochukwu, the human rights lawyer, informed us that arrangements had been concluded with ZAT television for live coverage of the tenure prolongation debate. "This," he said, "is one of our strategies to ensure that our constituents can differentiate between patriots and blacklegs as we debate the issue. It will not be a case of somebody who has swallowed half a million American dollars coming round to say he is against the Bill."

"But they can always run away from the debate," somebody said. Ogochukwu chuckled. "Precisely, everyone will answer his father's name. Let them run away from their ignoble cause. The more the merrier: those who run away from standing for the Bill for which they have swallowed such a huge amount of money will help our case. Their ranks will be thinned. Only the ringleaders will stay to answer the President's name."

The meeting was concluded by Hon. Kalkulus, who shared out more responsibilities.

"Hon. Angel, Yellow, Ibrahim and Dantata will accompany me to visit some of our former Presidents who are totally behind us in this matter. Hon. Samuel and Lizzy will follow up on the visit to the Labour Congress, while Chuks will complete his work on the analysis of the Bill. We need it for the interview on the CNN next week. We also want Socrates and Yetunde to …"

"Sorry, Leader," said a tall bearded Member from Jigawa. "We need to urgently address the issue of our security. Many of our colleagues, especially from States where our governors are in support of the Bill, are facing serious threats. Many of us are under 24-hour surveillance and harrassment by security agents.

We even have information that our houses have been bugged and we are not safe."

The Member's view were corroborated by other Members who had also experienced similar threats.

"I even get threatening phone calls daily, while two attempts have been made to kidnap my children," another Member observed.

"My Governor has even threatened to organise my recall," said a Member from Zamfara.

"My father in-law, who is very close to the President, has threatened to recall my wife," a Member from Gombe said, and the room erupted in laughter.

"Let him recall her. We shall get you two new wives," observed Hon. Chuks, known for his jokes. After the resultant laughter had gone down, the leader advised Members to be more serious with their security.

"We need to be wary of strange faces near our residences. We should also warn school authorities not to allow any unknown persons to come for our children after closing hours. It is also important that we don't go out alone whenever we go out late. Let me end by reminding us that we should all remain in Abuja till the end of this struggle. This is not the time to travel for any ceremony in your constitutuency or even abroad. Already, the government has started dishing out free tickets and mouth-watering offers to our Members to attend conferences in far-off countries. Apart from the danger of incessant travel, the idea is to get you out of the way so that when the debate starts it is only those on their side that will be counted. This is true because up till now the Speaker has not given us the exact date when the debate will commence. I therefore want to admonish you all to stay at your posts and keep safe. The good thing is that we have been able to gather a lot of information about the plans of the House Leadership on the project through moles whom we have planted in their midst," he said, as the meeting came to an end.

# CHAPTER

# 20

After the late-night meeting of our group, I gave Lizzy a ride to her house. She had excused her driver for the day, she said, and did not want to drive so late in the night. She invited me into her flat for a hot chocolate drink. Sitting relaxed in Lizzy's sitting room, I took off my cap. "My goodness," Lizzy exclaimed, "what happened to your head?"

"An accident," I said," a car accident." I had gone around in long-sleeve clothes and a cap since my discharge. That way, nobody saw anything and therefore nobody asked me any questions. I was beginning to feel uneasy. Perhaps I should have left my cap on.

Lizzy stared at me penetratingly. "A car accident? When? How?"

"Two weeks ago."

"But," she said, "your car is in perfect condition." Lizzy shot me a long quizzical look but I stood my ground.

"That's how much you know. I had an accident, pure and simple."

"Samuel, when did you start … I have always known you to be truthful; naïve, yes but truthful. Now, if you had had a car accident, the papers would carry it, the whole House would have heard. Tell me the truth, something else happened to you?"

"Sizzling Lizzy, the nosy parker. Tell me what else happened to me then," I challenged her.

"I hope … Sam … tell me the truth, did an irate husband catch you red-handed with his wife?"

I laughed and momentarily thrust aside the hot chocolate drink I had been enjoying. "What do you take me for, a reckless undisciplined sex maniac?"

Like wounds of war, requiring medals for heroism, I showed her the wounds on my arms and legs.

"Samuel," Lizzy said, "these are deliberate, not accidental, wounds. You don't get them from a traffic accident. My aunt, my guardian in secondary school, is a nurse and runs her own clinic. Wounds from accidents don't spare parts of the body."

So intent were her words and so sincere were her feelings that I finally told her the truth.

"Thank you, Honourable Samuel. Now I know lawyers never lie; they only hide the truth behind the facts. So what do you want to do with this girl after all this punishment?"

"I will marry her, of course."

"You will what? Honourable Samuel Lover-boy Bature, you will what? You were lucky they did not put a dagger in your heart. 'I will marry her, of course.' How suicidal can you get?"

"We are already engaged."

Lizzy stoop up and began to pace. "Engaged, to a Fulani? Engaged? Samuel, are you into hard drugs or what? Fulanis are very dangerous and of unpredictable temper. Now you barely escaped from their murderous hands … you cannot marry her, your name is a dead giveway. You are not even a Muslim."

"I will be converted in a few days' time," I said.

Lizzy threw her headgear off in a gesture of frustration. "Jesus! you will convert to Islam because of a girl … what is this phrase this Honourable used to use o?… *ah, ah*, I remember … nonsense on stilts … this is nonsense on stilts. Has the girl given you something to eat? Love potion inside *fura da nono*? You, Samuel, son of Bakura, descendant of two generations of Christians, reduced to a whimpering romantic mess by a nineteen-year-old girl? Converting to Islam?"

Suddenly the windows rattled, startling us both. But it was the wind turned noisy and aggressive. Lizzy got up to shutter her windows. Loud claps of thunder rang out. The room was bathed intermittently in the eerie blue of lightning.

"Oh, my goodness, another storm," I said, grabbing my cap and getting up to leave.

"You are going nowhere, lover-boy Samuel. I need to talk some sense into your broken head."

"But the rain, the storm …"

"Sit down, Mister Man. Which rain? I beg, it will soon stop." Lizzy moved nearer, and then sat by me on the settee, her smooth beautiful black hair glistening, its fragrance invading my nostrils. "Now this your Fulani brouhaha. You don't know what you are doing. You are suffering from love intoxication, grade-A infatuation. Listen, after one failed marriage, you want to rush heedless like a headless chicken into …" Suddenly, her mobile phone rang. "Yes, who?. Albert …which Albert?" she said, ringing off. "Samuel, the Fulani are headstrong, proud, violent and disdainful of non-Fulani. They are extremely reserved: you never know what a Fulani is thinking. This small girl of yours …"

She was again interrupted by her mobile phone. "Yes, what can I do for you, Albert? Services? Which services … you are … Okay, okay. Thanks, I am okay. I don't need your services." She looked angry and embarrassed.

"Who was that?" I asked. Lizzy shook her head in disgust, sighing deeply. "It's one of those ugly gigolos. He wanted to find out if I needed his services."

"Gigolo … what is a gigolo?"

"Come on, Samuel Bature, a whole lawyer like you and you don't know what a gigolo is?"

"Oh, oh … ah, those chaps who dole out sexual gratification for money. But are they in this country? Do they really exist?"

"Typical male chauvinist thinking. Why wouldn't they exist? If men run to female prostitutes for gratifi-cation, what makes you think that women won't summon male prostitutes for fulfilment?" Lizzy asked.

"Lizzy, so you patronize gigolos?"

"Of course not, you cloth-head. God forbid, who needs them? Not sizzling Lizzy, Honourable Member of the Fifth House of Representatives."

"But," I intervened," how come he has your number?"

"I don't know who gave him my number. The only thing I know is that two acquaintances of mine who work here in Abuja told me once they had retained the services of one or two gigolos. I will give them the full length of my tongue if they are the cloth-heads who …" She trailed off, angry, sullen, looking confused.

I felt in my bones that Lizzy was lying, but resisted the temptation to force the issue. I now had my own girl, a ravishing Fulani beauty, young and innocent, and Lizzy did not mean much to me any more. After a while I said, "This is serious. Why would those women need gigolos? Can't they find nice men for themselves?"

Lizzy stood up and opened the windows a bit. The rain had slowed to a peaceful drizzle. She began to speak. "Many rich single women keep gigolos. They hate to get involved with men who will give them a headache. Far cheaper, far safer, far, far more emotion-ally comfortable to have their needs met on demand. Paid for, no complications … ah, where were we before you came in, lover-boy lawyer, with the interlocutory injunction of gigolos? Forget this Fulani girl. Choose a wife with the full weight of your brains, not through a haze of *fura-da-nono* infatuation."

"Nobody can stop me," I said. "We are both in love. I am going ahead with the marriage. My Muslim name is …"

Lizzy took me by the shoulders and shook me vigorously. "Wake up, Samuel. It is a case of infatuation pure and simple." The rich aroma of Lizzy's expensive perfume was beginning to generate "infatuation" in me. I moved away – slightly.

*"Ehn,* Samuel, has it come to that?" she said, moving closer. "Lover-boy Samuel, now tell me the truth, you felt I was playing hard to get. Ha, ha, I was taking my time to study you well."

"Take my hand. We suit each other. I am ready," she said, playing with my hair, our hands clasped together as in a handshake.

"Lizzy, you don't need me, do you? You have enough men at your beck and call."

"Says who? Sammy, Sammy, don't you know those men you are referring to are birds of passage. Sammy dear ... I am ready to settle down ...with a compatible soul like you. We have so many things in common, I Lizzy and you, lover-boy, Samuel."

Outside, the rain had picked up again, as another clap of thunder rang out following a flash of lighting. Suddenly, the lights in the building went off in a power failure.

\* \* \*

It was almost two in the morning and the seven of us, Lizzy, Chuks, Yellow, Socrates, Angel, Kalkulus and I, were heading back to our cars through the gradually thinning revellers in Maitama Park. We had just finished a long celebratory dinner at one of the new restaurants in the park – a Mexican one called El Palacio. The Deputy Speaker had just turned forty and so he had decided to throw a bash for the honourable members. It was a big crowd with most of the members turning up with their spouses, some with their children.

It was the height of the acrimonious debate on the Tenure Prolongation Bill and the house was clearly divided. That was why we had decided to attend the party as a group since we couldn't trust any other person from another group.

El Palacio was one of the new wave of restaurants putting Abuja on the national gastronomic map. The walls were white and splashed with modern art. Soft jazz provided relief from the manic pace of the city outside. On the menu was avocado ravioli filled with shrimp mayonnaise spiked with chipotle, a smoken dried jalapeño pepper, followed by venison rubbed with Yucatán oregano amd dried burnt chillies served on puréed plantain. It was an exotic outing for me since I was not very adventurous when it came to food. And apart from tortilla, a thin, unleavened cake of fresh cornmeal dough which I had had about a year ago in a Mexican restaurant in Lagos, I had not thought myself a great fan of Mexican food.

"The event must have cost the DS a lot of money," I observed to Lizzy, who was in an eye-popping black lentil suit. "I wonder why he had to spend so much on an ordinary birthday," I added.

"What's ordinary? I have told you that you still have a lot to learn in politics," Lizzy replied. "The DS is preparing for his State's governorship election. That's why he invited all the 'who's who' in the society."

Despite the hour, we all agreed to have a short meeting before retiring to bed. The debate on the controversial Bill was to commence in two weeks and we needed to fine-tune our strategies. This became all the more urgent in view of the 100,000 dollar bribe already being circulated among the Members. Although many had collected the money, it had not ensured the two-thirds majority needed for the passage of the Bill. All the same, it was our decision to meet and perfect our tactics in ensuring that the Bill did not see the light of the day.

And so it was that we all headed to Honourable Socrates' house in Zone E for the meeting, which was presided over as usual by Honourable Kalkulus.

"Samuel, can you please give us an update of the expected voting pattern?" Kalkulus asked.

I quickly brought out a sheet of paper from the inner pocket of my *babariga* and read from my analysis.

"Out of the six geopolitical zones, our greatest strength are in the North-West and North-East, where many Members are opposed to the Tenure Prolongation Bill since they had expected to produce the next president. Our weakest chain still remains South-South and South-East. We can only count about ten votes from these two zones."

"Can you give us a rough analysis of the number of votes on both sides?" Socrates asked.

"As of yesterday, we had ninety confirmed votes while they have 190. For the bill to pass, they need two-thirds of 360, which is 240."

"That means they need 90 more votes," Lizzy observed.

"While we need just 30 more."

"I can't see them getting 90 votes in two weeks," Honourable Yellow, ever an incurable optimist, observed.

"Don't say that," Hon. Kalkulus said. "Two weeks is a long time in politics. Anything can happen."

The room was quiet for a while as we were all engrossed in our thoughts. Kalkulus once again broke the silence.

"Anyway that is by the way; our immediate problem is a motion that will be heard later this morning. It is a motion to pass a vote of confidence in the President."

"When was the motion slated? It wasn't in our weekly order paper," Hon. Angel said.

"No it wasn't. It was smuggled in late yesterday. I only got to know just before the DS birthday party," Kalkulus said.

"Vote of confidence? Of what benefit will that be to them? I may be wrong, but I don't see it as a motion we should be afraid of," Yellow said.

"No Yellow, you have come again," Chuks shouted. "You always find it difficult to adequately read your opponent. It is a very tactical motion. It is a precursor to the Tenure Prolongation Bill. The idea is to propagate all the President's achievements and lionise him as irreplaceable. This way, the ground for his continued stay in power will be guaranteed."

"Who is moving the motion?' Socrates asked.

"Who else but Okoro, the Chief Whip? He always does their dirty work for them," Chuks replied.

"In addition to what Chuks has just said," Hon Kalkulus said," the motion is also an attempt by the leadership to test the waters for the Tenure Prolongation Bill. Furthermore, I understand that the second tranche of the half-million-dollar bribe has arrived for the pro-third-term Members. And the only way by which the money could be released is for the leadership to show their sponsors how much work they have done with the first tranche. It is expected that voting will go the way of the third-term position. The leadership want to impress their sponsors and so the secretary behind the motion. A win for them, they believe, is a win for the third-term agenda. Our duty is to frustrate their plans."

"Apart from impressing their sponsors, if the motion sails through, it could send the wrong signal to other members who are still sitting on the fence and tilt them to join the other side. It could also dampen the spirit of our supporters as well as our Members," our leader observed.

"But what can we do at this late hour? Unlike us, they could have had time to mobilize their Members," asked Lizzy, who had all the while been dozing beside me.

"In addition," I added, "some of our Members may not be around and may not be able to contribute to the debate."

After a long discussion, it was agreed that Chuks and I should prepare a handbill enumerating reasons why a vote of confidence in the President should not be passed. The handbill to be placed in Members' mailboxes as early as possible, while more would be distributed in the chambers.

"If you can get the handbills ready on time, I can distribute them to the residences of the Members before they leave for the Chamber," Hon Socrates said. "To me, this is a very important project. The motion must be stopped by all means. I am ready to do door-to-door evangelism," he added as we all burst into laughter.

"In addition to the handbills, we need to get more Members of our group to talk during the debate," Lizzy observed.

"We have to select good and influential speakers."

"You are right, Lizzy," Kalkulus said.

We later agreed on those to argue against the motion.

Kalkulus was given the task of informing those concerned before the commencement of debate.

"What about our plan B?" Chuks asked.

"Plan B? What is that?" I asked.

"Something to fall back on in case our initial plan fails. These people are desperate to win the motion. The Speaker may not allow our Members to speak or he may want to sway the votes for the motion whatever our Members might say. We therefore need to plan for that," Chuks said.

"What do you have in mind? Kalkulus asked.

"We can stop the debate!"

"You mean filibustering?" Socrates asked.

"Yes," Chuks said.

"And how do you want to do that? What House order will you quote to stop the debate?"

"No, we don't need any House order. All we need is to throw the chamber into confusion and prevent the motion from being heard."

"By stealing the mace?" Lizzy asked.

"No, we won't steal the mace like Wenike did. Samuel and I have done it before. We can make noise and raise enough hell to prevent the debate from proceeding. I also have some connection with the technical staff. We can cut off the power supply or stop the air conditioning system working."

"We can also short circuit the microphones," I added.

"How will you do that?" Angel asked.

"Leave that to Chuks and me."

"Finally," Hon Kalkulus said, "information has reached us that the President sent emissaries to some African countries to seek their support for the tenure prolongation agenda. From reports, some of these leaders have promised their support while others are yet to decide. Our friends have therefore advised that we also need to reach out to some of these leaders in order to put things in proper perspective. Just yesterday, I was informed that a conference on the African Peer Review Mechanism will hold next week in Uganda. Several African leaders will be attending and it will be a good opportunity for us to present our case. Our friends in the diplomatic corps have promised to assist us in Kampala next week."

"What about the funds for the trip?" Lizzy asked.

"Again, our friends are ready to sponsor three of us."

Kalkulus said, "Since we are in a very crucial period, we don't want to be all out of town. I am therefore proposing that Samuel, Effiong and I go for the trip so that Socrates, Chuks and the rest will man the front in our absence."

# CHAPTER

# 21

The Public Hearing for my Bill, *A Bill for an Act to Establish a Commission for Pastoralists and Agri-culturalists in Nigeria*, was a huge success. Since the official period for sitting was in the afternoon on Wednesdays, the hearing was fixed for ten in the morning. Despite my suggestion that they should arrive Abuja on the preceeding Tuesday, members of the Fulani community decided to travel all night on Tuesday and arrive in Abuja early in the morning. However, members of the Farmers' Union, especially those from the southern part of the country, had arrived the previous day.

I was particularly happy to see Batejo once again. Since my discharge from the hospital after the assault by Gidado and his friends, I had seen her only once, when I went to give the Fulani community their transport money.

I found her in the midst of her people as they dissembarked from the lorry that had brought them from Bauchi. As usual, she was stunning in her red brassière, green tunic and yellow sash outfit. With her dark braided hair cascading to her shoulders, she appeared utterly enchanting in the early morning sunshine.

"You look so lovely," I told her as I helped her up the stairways from the car park in front of the White House venue of the public hearing. The assorted colorful dress of the Fulanis blending radiantly with the white *galabiyas* of the Hausa farmers and the dark suits of the officials from government agencies and those from Development Partners and NGOs. In view of the importance of the Bill and the massive publicity given the event, a battery of journalists occupied a corner of the room.

As I entered the room, I quickly called Batejo aside and handed her the memorandum which I had typed for her on two sheets of paper.

"You need to go through it before the event commences," I said as I drew up two chairs for both of us.

Once I had confirmed that she was conversant with what I had written for her, I allowed her to join her group while I continued with the other arrangements for the event.

Gradually, the room filled up with people. I was glad to see my friends from the conference that I had attended in Lagos. Apart from Professor Ahmed, there was also Dr Albert along with a few other university professors. They were followed by members of the Committees on Agriculture, Conflict Resolution and Human Rights, who were the main sponsors of the Bill.

Finally, the Speaker arrived, accompanied by some of the House Leaders. On seeing members of his contituency who had come for the event, the Speaker broke protocol and came down from the High Table to greet them. Although most of his constitutents were the town Fulanis, who had little or nothing to do with cattle rearing, they came in large numbers.

Much against tradition, the Speaker decided to stay back to witness the proceedings after the initial introductions. It was obvious that he did this more out of political considerations than out of interest.

Batejo was fantastic in her presentation. Due to the long rehearsal I had had with her, her memorandum on behalf of the Fulani cattle rearers was well received.

In her conclusion, Batejo observed thus: "As a very important player in the food chain production in the country, we the nomadic Fulani would appreciate more support from the government. In this respect, we want the government to create a North-South grazing corridor for our cattle which will be devoid of interference by farmers or security guards. In addition, as taxpayers, we would appreciate more meaningful government presence in our lives, such as better veterinary services for our cattle, provision of boreholes in our *rigas* and along our grazing routes, and motorable roads to transport our cattle to the market. We want more and better equipped nomadic schools as well as maternity centres to cater for our pregnant women."

In their own memorandum, presented by Alhaji Meguda, the President of the Farmers' Association, the farmers wanted government to relax the land use decree promulgated several years ago by the military in order to make it easy for them to access more land for farming purposes. They also wanted government to provide farming implements such as tractors as well as fertilizers at affordable rates. In addition, they wanted government to assist them in selling their farm products through co-operatives. They also wanted compensation for the assorted damage they had suffered in the hands of the Fulani. In his conclusion, Alhaji Meguda said: "While we have nothing against the provision of a North-South grazing corridor for the Fulani cattle rearers, it is important that this corridor be far away from our farmlands and well demarcated. This way the incessant encroachment on our farmlands by the Fulani which is actually the main cause of friction will be totally eradicated or at least much reduced."

Due to the good groundwork I had done, the public hearing ended in an amicable way. As I saw off Batejo and her people, she quickly whispered to me that she would be spending the weekend with her elder sister in Abuja. This was good news and I promised to check on her as soon as I could get away from work.

When the last guests had departed the venue of the public hearing, I went on to the chamber to attend the day's proceedings. I arrived in time just as the Speaker announced the first order of the day.

"The first order of the day is a motion on the missing Nigerian Communications Satellite (NigComSat), which got lost in space about two weeks ago, in the name of Hon. Mohammed Sanusi and ten others. I now call on Hon. Mohammed Sanusi to present his motion."

Hon. Mohammed Sanusi, also the Chairman, House Committee on Science and Technology, was a tall ramrod-thin young man from Katsina State. Having been given a local chieftaincy title of Turaki, he was known to wear a green turban which always contrasted sharply with his white *babariga*. He quickly finished chewing a piece of kola nut which had been in his mouth for a while. Then, from a sheet of paper in his hands, he read: "Mr. Speaker, my colleagues, I thank you for giving me the opportunity to present my motion, which is very important but unfortunately very embarrassing and sad. You will all recall that two years ago, at the inception of this house, we all celebrated with fanfare and pomp the launching of Nigeria's first satellite in faraway China. The project, which was executed for National Space Research and Development Agency by the China Great Wall Industry Corporation, cost the Federal Government of Nigeria a whopping N40 billion. The satellite, which has four gateways located in South Africa, China and Italy, was supposed to improve internet access to even the remotest rural villages and to enhance government's economic reforms in the areas of e-learning, e-commerce, tele-medicine and tele-education among others.

"Although the satellite was said to have a lifespan of 15 years, it had since packed up. Mr. Speaker, Honourable Members, the most disturbing develop-ment is the inconsistency in the pronounce-ments of government officials since the satellite's disappearance. While some ministry officials denied that the satellite was missing, officials of NigComSat claimed that the satellite was only faulty and not missing. In view of this, Honourable Speaker and my colleagues, this motion has the following prayers:

"That the Managing Director of NigComsat, Alhaji Baba

Salihu, be summoned to face the Committee on Science and Technology to explain his company's role in this very embarrassing incident.

"That the House, through its Committee on Science and Technology, investigate the claims that the quality of the material used for the satellite was substandard and, even if of good quality, was not meant for Africa but for Asian countries.

"That the House Committee on Science and Technology investigate whether or not the satellite was insured.

"Finally, that members of the House Committee on Science and Technology proceed on a fact-finding mission to China to investigate the remote and recent causes of the lost satellite."

Hon. Sanusi's presentation was followed by other contributions all agreeing with the prayers of the motion. Just as the Speaker was about to bang the gavel to pass the motion, a hand suddenly shot up on the right-hand side of the chamber.

"Yes, Honourable?" the Speaker said.

"My name is Honourable Ahmed. I represent Jigawa Central constituency. I wish to seek for an amendment in the last prayer of the motion: instead of members visiting China, they should go to space, since it was in space that the satellite disappeared. The only problem is how to get a visa to visit space and …" As he said this, the whole chamber rocked with laughter.

"Space? How will you get there?" one member shouted.

"Visa? To where?" another shouted as more laughter engulfed the chamber.

Despite this show of derision, Honourable Aminu remained resolute. "Mr. Speaker, am I protected?" Even at that, it took another five minutes or so before quiet and order finally descended on the chamber.

Immediately after the Speaker had brought sanity back to the house, Honourable Ahmed Aminu was back on his feet with his request for amendment that the Honourable Members should visit space instead of China. He even put the amendment in writing and passed it to the Speaker. The Speaker, knowing the mood of the house on the matter, quickly took charge.

"I will first of all put the question on Hon Aminu's amendment which now becomes prayer No 5. It says that 'In view of the fact that the satellite in question went missing in space, Members of the House Committee on Science and Technology should visit space rather than China.' Is there any seconder to the amendment?"

The whole House erupted into No! No! No!

Since there was no seconder to the amendment, the Speaker quickly ruled on the main motion, which was quickly resolved.

As the Speaker was about to continue with the day's proceedings, another hand shot up. Although the next item was very important, the Speaker had no choice but to recognise the Member, a tall, dark elderly man with a greying beard.

"My name is Hon. Abubakar Yahaya, representing the good people of Suleja, Gurara and Tafa Federal constituency. Mr Speaker, I am coming under order V rules 1, 2 and 3 of our standing orders on matters of privilege. Yesterday, there was a press conference by Hon. Rimi where he accused this House of taking bribes before passing the budget. He also called this House a beer parlour. In fact, many newspapers have reported this issue. The report is in *The Sun, The Daily Independent, The AM Express, The Mail* and *The Champion*. It was also reported on the BBC Hausa service.

"Mr. Speaker, this House, as far as we know, has not taken any bribe to pass the budget. Moreover, this House is not a beer parlour. To my mind, what Hon. Rimi has done has badly damaged the reputation of this House and I request that we suspend him and refer this matter to the Ethics and Privileges Committee to take up this matter. I so move."

*Hon. Olukemi Olurin (Oyo Central):* Mr. Speaker sir, I wish to second the motion.

*Hon. Ahmed Shehu (Bauchi Central):* Mr. Speaker, in all morality, in all responsiveness, any sane person cannot come up with these kinds of allegations on national television that our debates are beer parlour debates. Hon. Rimi has been here for four years. Let him bring whatever he has brought in form of debates on this floor of the House. Let him tell us any input that he has made for one day to better the people who elected him. We are honourable people and we cannot in all sincerity allow one of us, one from among us to see us and paint us black. In fact, what Rimi has done is to embark on a coup against this parliament. This is in summary what he intends to happen and we tell Rimi thus: "Mr. Rimi, we have a future ahead of us. If you think you do not have a future, we have a future in this political dispensation and we guard it jealously."

Hon. Shehu's submission was greeted with wild applause.

*Hon. James Oguka (Delta North):* Thank you, Mr Speaker. It is a very sad thing to see one of us trying to destroy this House. What our colleague has done since yesterday is indeed sacrilegious. He has murdered sleep in my own view and he should be gated. First, I think he has brought shame on himself, to his family and indeed on his constituency. Secondly, he has brought shame on his party. My suggestion is that we hand him over to his party for appropriate discipline.

*Hon. Bayo Iluku (Lagos Central):* Mr. Speaker, honourable colleagues, I don't see what is wrong in Hon. Rimi's statement except that he was too blunt. Let's be honest with ourselves: when you allow television cameras into the parliament you allow the public to see us as we are. The impression given to the public by the near-empty chamber is that we are a bunch of unserious people when, in actual fact, many Members are busy with other parliamentary jobs, such as oversight functions, committee meetings and constituency visits. More confusing are our obscure procedures, arcane language and excruciating tedium. The farmyard noises and occasional fisticuffs that we see in the Chamber make the business of democracy seem cheap. Over a century ago, Lord Curzon described the British Parliament as 'the playground of jesters and the paradise of bores'. This to me has not changed much and that is exactly what Hon Rimi is trying to say, maybe too bluntly, but we …

*Members:* No! No! No! Sit down, Sit down!

*The Speaker:* Hon. Members, please: we are dealing with a serious issue and I do not want us to discuss it on party lines or in terms of personal sentiments. So, please, we have run this House as a family and if one of your children errs and you are punishing him, it does not mean that you do not like him, you are punishing him because he needs correction; so we should try not to see the issues in the light of the way some people are trying to portray it. We are all responsible people here, and so we must act responsibly. I will therefore appeal to my colleague Hon. Abubakar Yahaya who started this whole issue to conclude.

*Hon. Abubakar Yahaya:* Mr. Speaker, thank you very much for giving me the opportunity to speak again. I raised this issue and, with all the contributions from our members, I will once again recommend that we suspend Hon. Rimi for one month to allow the Ethics and Privileges Committee to carry our its duties and I move that the question be put.

The Speaker quickly put the question and went ahead to suspend Hon. Rimi for one month to allow the Ethics and Privileges Committee to carry out its duty. The committee later announced its verdict: Hon. Rimi was suspended without pay for three months for denigrating the hallowed Chamber of the Nigerian Parliament.

"The next order for today is the motion calling for a vote of confidence on the President, Federal Republic of Nigeria, in the name of the House Leader and one hundred other members."

As the Speaker said this, half of the chamber hissed while the other half cheered.

In his seat at the left upper part of the chamber, Hon. Kalkulus flashed me a V-sign. I in turn looked around for Hon. Chuks. I saw him at the left lower part of the Chamber, still circulating the handbills we had distributed in the morning. He too gave me a thumbs-up. As I gazed round the chamber, I was relieved to see members of our group present and ready for action. I took out a piece of copper wire from the inner pocket of my jacket and connected one end to the wire of my microphone and the other to Elizabeth's microphone. With this in place, I switched on the microphone and suddenly, the Speaker's voice was cut off. Satisfied that the experiment was successful, I removed the wire and redirected my attention to the House leader, who was now moving his motion.

"Dear colleagues, we all know that the President has done extremely well; apart from unemployment and inflation rates which are at their lowest rates in years, the country continues to enjoy an enormous amount of peace and tranquility. It is also on record that the ..."

Suddenly the lights went off and the cooling system stopped working.

"Oh no!" came cries from every section of the chamber.

Since it normally takes a few minutes for the alternative source of power to be switched on during power outages, we all waited for the power to be on. However, when five minutes turned to ten and the interior of the Chamber was getting stuffy, the Clerk and the Sergeant-at-Arms quickly scurried out to see what was amiss.

During the confusion and waiting, Chuks sidled up to me, grinning from ear to ear.

"Our boys have struck," he said as we pumped hands.

"But how long can they keep it up?" I asked.

"Thirty minutes at best, but it can be repeated. By the time the same thing has happened three times, the Speaker will be forced to adjourn."

As we talked, the lights and the cooling system came on.

"Just twenty minutes," Chuks said.

"Not bad," I commented.

The leader had only got about five minutes into his speech when the lights went off again.

This time, power was restored within ten minutes. The Speaker, now suspecting foul play, instructed the clerk to immediately change the technicians at the control centre with a new team.

After the leader's speech, other contributors spoke, all endorsing the fantastic performance of the President.

Naturally, the speeches were followed by loud applauses. Fearing that if the trend continued, we might find it difficult to garner enough support to counter the motion, Chuks quickly signalled to me showing me two fingers, indicating that I should put into action our second plan.

I quickly fished out the tiny copper wire from my pocket and again connected my microphone with Elizabeth's. For a few seconds, nothing happened then suddenly the voice of the Member making the speech gradually fizzled out and all we heard was a dull ringing tone that floated round the chambers as the copper wire shortcircuited the sound system.

Once again, the House was thrown into commo-tion as some Members hissed while others applauded. The Speaker, eager to bring sanity to the chamber, frantically slapped his microphone and when he couldn't get any sound, beckoned the clerk, who in turn summoned the Sergeant-at-Arms, who quickly trotted out of the chamber in search of the technicians.

In my seat, I used my knees to keep the copper wire in place while trying to appear as if nothing was happening. Apart from Chuks and Lizzy, nobody knew that I was the cause of the interruption. After ten minutes the Sergeant-at-Arms reappeared to test the microphones. When they did not work, he again disappeared.

Another ten minutes passed before he reappeared with an overalled technician, who insisted that the fault was from the Chamber.

Together with the other Chamber stewards, the two proceeded from pew to pew glancing down to see if they could notice anything amiss.

Sitting comfortably in my seat, I kept my eyes innocently on a newspaper which hid my knees from where they propped up the copper wire.

That was how I was missed.

Twenty minutes later, when the cause of the fault in the sound system could not be detected, the Speaker had no choice but to adjourn the sitting till ten the following morning to the cheers of members of our group and the jeers from the pro-government Members.

# CHAPTER

# 22

I found Batejo waiting for me where we had arranged. It had been difficult for me to get away from the chambers after the adjournment. Chuks and two other members of our group whom Chuks had informed about the cause of the microphone failure were all over me once we left the chambers.

As they continued to congratulate me in loud voices, I quickly cautioned them not to let out the secret since we might still have to use the same trick at a later date.

Despite Lizzy's pleas that I escort her to the accounts section to check her outstanding payments, I had to quickly rush into my car for the half-hour drive to the busy Wuse market where I had arranged to meet Batejo.

It was interesting that since she discovered my interest in Batejo, Lizzy had been doing her best to get closer. I was, however, determined to be faithful to Batejo, so I did my best to avoid her. Rather than go back to Bauchi with her group after the public hearing, Batejo and I had arranged for her to stay with her sister for two more days. I had phoned her to meet me at the kiosk close to her sister's fashion shop where we could have a brief talk.

"What took you so long? I thought you were not coming again," she asked, her eyes dancing with joy at the sight of me. Batejo was still wearing the bright red brassière and tunic which she had worn to the public hearing. Her braided silky hair, richly decorated with colourful beads, still fell deliciously down to her shoulders. She looked as ravishing as she had always been. Now, with the joy of my coming, her lovely dark large eyes were much livelier.

"You look very beautiful, my love. I like your permed hair, it is just magical," I said as I looked deep into her face, drinking in the beauty before me.

"I didn't perm my hair, I only rubbed it with *manshanu*," said Batejo, laughing a little, indignantly but delightfully.

"*Manshanu*? What is that?"

"It is the cheese we get from the yogurt we make from fresh milk. It makes our hair shine and also keeps it fresh and wards off flies and insects."

"It's beautiful and I feel like touching it."

"No, don't," she said, laughing. "My sister may see us."

"So what? Have you not told her yet?"

She shook her head. "She's too conservative. She won't accept us. I am waiting for my uncle to tell her. That way, it will be easier to convince her."

I bought two cans of coke and passed one to her. She shook her head. "I prefer *zobo*, coke is too sweet for me."

"That makes two of us – I also prefer *zobo*." I negotiated an exchange with the kiosk operator.

The *zobo* came, we sipped it and talked to each other about how the public hearing went, about the gaily dressed Fulani whose bright colours interspersed so well with those of the Hausa farmers. I was impressed with the ease with which Batejo spoke about serious issues of politics, religion and the economy. It was amazing that, in spite of her bucolic background, her grasp of current national issues was excellent. We also spoke about the weather, how very different the humid Abuja was to the cool hills and mountains of Bauchi. She spoke freely and gaily as we quietly sipped our drinks. Suddenly, she leaned closer, staring deeply into my eyes, and said, "I forgot to tell you how handsome you look in that suit."

"Thanks, I didn't know you would like it. Never knew you like western clothes."

"I do, only that I am not allowed to wear them."

"You will, my dear, when we get married."

"And when will that be?" she asked, chuckling.

"Once we get over these problems in the house, you know I told you about this third-term bill. The stupid thing is causing so much tension, especially for those of us against it. We are under serious security surveillance. It is bad enough for me having to watch my back. I don't want to endanger your life by marrying you now. In another month or two, it should be over; then I will feel safer to have you to myself." She smiled, a sweet broad smile that lit up her pretty face. She shook her bottle of zobo to avoid letting the thick purple drink settle.

"Please be careful, Sammy. Don't be too critical. I don't want the authorities to harm you."

"I will my dear – I will …"

Just then a light-complexioned lady like an older version of Batejo came over to where we were sitting. Frowning and without greeting me, she spoke in Fulfulde to Batejo.

As the lady later walked away, Batejo quickly got up.

"That was my sister, she wants me to help with the packing up. The shop is about to close for the day."

"She didn't look too happy to see me," I said.

Batejo smiled, a reassuring smile as she quickly finished her drink. "It's normal for her to behave that way. I told you, she is very conservative. Don't worry, as soon as you are ready with your cows and the flogging ceremony, she will take a good liking to you."

"Which flogging? After Gidado and his friends almost killed me? Anyway, when do we see each other again; is tomorrow okay?"

"No, I go back to Bauchi tomorrow … and …"

"But I … I … thought you wouldn't go back until the day after tomorrow?"

"That was what I thought myself until my sister told me of a wedding in the *riga* the day after tomorrow."

"Oh what a pity," I said. "That means I shan't see you for two weeks. I'm travelling to Uganda next week for a conference."

"Uganda, that's in East Africa."

"Yes, your geography is good."

"How I wish I could come with you; but it's not possible for now."

"Don't worry, dear, there will always be plenty of time to go anywhere we want to," I said as she hurried back to her sister's shop.

As Batejo got to the shop, her sister Adama was already angry. "What kept you so long? You know we have to leave this place by six and it's already half past five. It takes time to bring in all these clothes you know?"

"I'm sorry, *Inna*, I will be fast," Batejo said as she started putting away the clothes.

"Who is that man?" Adama asked.

"Just a friend."

"Just a friend? And you were so deep in discussion you were almost kissing each other?"

"Ha ha, *Inna*," Batejo said, calling her sister the respectful name which showed that she was named after her grandparents.

"What is 'Ha ha, *Inna*'? You were so engrossed in your discussion you didn't even hear me call your name until I had to walk down to where you were sitting. What kind of friend is he? He looks far older than you and much too smooth for my liking." Adama said, her voice quivering with restrained anger.

Without waiting for an answer, she asked: "What is his name?"

"Sammy."

"Sammy what?"

Batejo hesitated; she knew that once her sister got Sammy's full name, more problems would crop up. She kept quiet and went on with the packing.

"I'm still waiting to know your friend's name." Adama said moments later.

"Sammy Bakura," Batejo said and waited for the worst.

"Sammy? That's not a Fulani name – it even sounds like a nickname. What's his real name, or have you something to hide?"

"His name is Samuel Bakura."

Adama suddenly stopped packing and looked up.

"Samuel? That's a Christian name."

"Yes, it is," Batejo replied weakly.

"Since when did we start befriending Christians in our family? Where is he from?"

"He is a *Gwagi* from Kaduna State."

"And if I may ask, what does he do for a living?"

Again, Batejo hesitated but her sister was insistent.

"He is a politician," Batejo said a few seconds later.

"*Subhanallah! Kai*, you mean, not only are you befriending a Christian, the fellow is also a politician, those dangerous and unreliable characters? I knew it when I saw him. The fellow is too smooth for my liking. Thank God he is only a friend. The earlier you get rid of him the better. Go and look for a better friend who is not only Fulani but also a Muslim and with a better job, not a cut-throat politician."

Suddenly, Batejo, unhappy with the derogatory way her sister was describing Samuel, wanted to stand up for him. This feeling gave her a little more strength and her mouth suddenly took a defiant set.

"Samuel may not be a Muslim or a Fulani, but he is a very decent man and I want to marry him."

Batejo's last words hit Adama so badly that the set of clothes she had been carrying fell from her hands in a heap at her feet. She clutched at her head, opened her mouth in silent horror, used her handkerchief to mop the sweat that had suddenly appeared on her brow and sat down.

"What about Gidado? I thought you are already engaged to him," she asked weakly.

"We used to be, but that is over now. Samuel is the man I want to spend the rest of my life with," Batejo replied a little more confidently.

"*Subbahanallh! Kai Subhanallah!*" Adama repeated as she picked up an old newspaper from the floor and started fanning herself, "What kind of madness has come over you? You left a young decent and hardworking Fulani boy like Gidado for this Gwagi Christian who is almost old enough to be your father? On top of it all, he is a politician, somebody who cannot be trusted for anything. Only God knows how many wives and girlfriends the fellow already has."

"He's not married," Batejo answered.

"That's what he told you; you mean at his age, he is still a bachelor? Oh, Batejo, an unmarried elderly man is a fox to be wary of, but wait until you get to his house; then you will see how many women have children for him already. Ha, what kind of *wahala* is this? A beautiful Fulani girl like you going to marry this dangerous specimen of humanity. Is this what they taught you at the nomadic school you attended? If I had known that this would be the result of education, I would have advised against it. I thought I was doing you a favour when I encouraged baba to send you to school. I never knew you would go there and learn nonsense. By the way, I thought Gidado had already paid four cows to the family. What will happen now?"

"Samuel will return his cows," Batejo answered.

"I see, I can now understand, it's all about money. No wonder, because this Tammy or Sammy is very rich, that's why you abandoned Gidado, *ehn?* Is that how we were brought up? To love money over good name?"

Batejo had by then stopped packing the clothes and sat down.

"*Inna,* you don't understand, it has nothing to do with money. I just love Sammy. You too will like him when you get to know him. He is a very decent and nice man. He was a lawyer before going into politics and …"

"Ha … ha … a lawyer, that's even worse," Adama interjected, "When you combine a lawyer with a politician in the same person, the only thing you can get is an armed robber. But you were so much in love with Gidado. Suddenly, Gidado is not good again. Because you are educated, you think you are too big to marry a cattle rearer? It is a politician that now suits you? May Allah help you," Adama said as she continued her job of packing away the clothes into the shop.

* * *

I was the toast of our meeting when our group met at the Hotel Tributary at Wuse Zone 8 later that evening. We decided to change the venue of our meeting just to throw off the security men who had been trailing us these past few days.

Although every member of our group soon got to know that I was responsible for the microphone's technical hitch, it was only Chuks and Lizzy who knew the technical details. Almost everybody was happy that we were able to filibuster the meeting, apart from Hon. Socrates, who thought that we should have allowed the debate to proceed since in his opinion we could have eventually defeated the motion if the house had divided as we expected.

"At any rate, we have only postponed the evil day because, come tomorrow, the matter will be tabled again and…" However, he was cut short by Honourable Kalkulus.

"It won't be tomorrow, it was just announced that the ruling party has an emergency meeting tomorrow and so there won't be any sitting tomorrow."

"But then if it's some time next week we can't run away from that debate," Socrates observed.

"Next week has been devoted for oversight visits while the debate on the Third Term Bill will commence the week after," Kalkulus said.

"That's good. So it's like their motion to shore up the President's image has finally being halted. That's good work that Chuks and Samuel did," said Honourable Angel.

Just then, Chuks entered the venue of the meeting breathlessly. He collapsed in one of the settees in a fit of laughter.

"What happened to you?" Hon. Yinusa asked.

Chuks continued laughing for a while before he finally spoke. "As I was rushing here for the meeting I saw a van parked by the side of the road adjacent to the Senate President's House. Standing by the van were Hon. Sheriff from Borno State as well as our dear friend Hon. Edobor from Edo and another Honourable member from Jigawa. I was just eager to get here on time but the trio had recognised my car and flagged me to a halt. That was when Sheriff started pleading with me to support the Tenure Prolongation Bill, saying that I would be well taken care of. The other two Members also joined in appealing to me, saying that we need continuity for stability in the country. When they saw that their pleas had no effect on me, Sheriff flung open the door of the van and showed me bags of American dollar bills neatly stacked from the floor to the roof. Each bag I was told contained 100,000 dollars. I was asked to take a bag and sign the register. When I refused, they offered me two bags."

"That's 200,000 dollars!" Honourable Yellow shouted.

"So what did you do?" Honourable Angel asked.

"I told them to return it to the sender; that the bill won't sail through," Chuks answered.

"*Ehn ehn*, so what's funny in that?" Honourable Socrates angrily asked Chuks, "Is this the first time you've been offered money? Two weeks ago, I was offered 200,000 dollars for this project; I refused and I didn't mention it to anybody, so what's the big deal in your own case?"

"Actually, why I was laughing was that Hon. Edobor had

collected a bag of money but he didn't want me to see it, so he quickly dropped it in a nearby dustbin. So when I asked him to accompany me to this meeting, he said he wanted to pick up something at home first. I had already seen him hiding the bag in the dustbin; so I insisted on taking him to his house so that we could come here together, but he still declined because he wanted to retrieve the money. I therefore pretended to be coming here but took another road that led back to the van. It was while I was coming back that I caught him getting the bag of money from the dustbin; so I went to him and asked him why he took the money. He started begging me not to tell this meeting, saying that it was his constituents who forced him to take the money. I promised not to tell anybody as long as he does not show his face in our meeting again. Just as I arrived in the Hall, he called me on my mobile and promised to give me 20,000 dollars if I don't tell anybody what happened. That's what caused my laughter."

"This is very serious, for somebody who calls himself a human rights lawyer," said Honourable Sheriff from Nasarawa.

"He's no more Human Rights but Human Rice," Lizzy said, and the room again dissolved in laughter.

After we had reviewed the plans for the tenure prolongation debate that was to take place in two weeks' time, Hon. Kalkulus informed the House that three of us, he, Hon. Effiong and I, would be going to Uganda over the weekend to attend the meeting of the African Peer Review Mechanism where we hoped to alert other African leaders to the Tenure Prolongation Bill.

The meeting was coming to a close when my mobile phone rang and a voice asked me to hold on for 'His Excellency'. It was the Governor of my State, Alhaji Salisu Mohammed. He wanted me to see him for something urgent the following day in Kaduna. Since we did not belong to the same political party, I was unsure of why he wanted to see me.

"I am sure he will try and convince you to vote for the Tenure Prolongation Bill," Hon. Chuks said, "Almost all the Governors are now busy trying to woo their legislators to sign for the Bill. In fact, I was reliably informed that the Presidency has even transferred the dollar bribe money to the Governors who they believe are more effective in persuading the recalcitrant Members to play ball."

"In that case, I won't go," I said.

"No, you have to go, party or no party, he is your Governor and you need to respect him," Honourable Socrates said, "What I can do for you is to give you this gadget," he said, taking out what looked like a wristwatch from his bag. "This is a high-tech video camera and recorder in one. Just strap it on like a wristwatch and you will have everything on record and we can have your Governor on tape, he concluded."

\* \* \*

I arrived at Government House, Kaduna early the following morning to keep the appointment with my State Governor, Alhaji Salisu Mohammed, a former civil engineer. For security reasons, I decided to travel during the day and so I had left Abuja about seven that morning. I found him waiting for me in his tastefully-furnished sitting room in a casual white *galabiya* and a white skullcap which further accentuated his youthful looks.

As we exchanged greetings, I quickly flipped on the switch of the wristwatch the way Hon. Socrates had instructed.

"Hon. Bakura, I am so happy you could come," the Governor said as he led me to his study, "I know you are a very busy man, so I won't keep you long." A servant rolled in a table loaded with food and drinks.

"We can talk as we eat ... ehm ... ehm ... I have bread, *kosai*, *kunu* and yam; what will you like?"

"The *kunu* and *kosai* will be okay," I said, remembering to raise up my hand so that the wristwatch would take a good picture of the 45-year-old man and his surroundings.

As we served ourselves, Alhaji said, "I have been hearing all the good things you have been doing in the House, especially this Bill on the nomadic Fulani and the settlers. I hope it will be passed quickly. Our people have suffered too much from these ravaging Fulani. Well done, Honourable, it's a very good Bill."

"Thank you, Your Excellency," I replied.

The Governor popped a ball of *kosai* in his mouth and chewed for a while before speaking.

"I also know your position on this tenure prolongation bill. It is not as if some of us like the Bill, but we need to go along with the President to avoid being victimised. I am sure you know what is happening to some of my Governor colleagues who openly criticised the bill? One of them has been impeached while the other is fighting for his life after thugs took over the state capital. Another, as you know, was arrested on a tip-off in Germany for currency trafficking. You know, in politics, self-preservation is the first rule, so we need to safeguard our jobs first. It is after that that you can help others. Once you lose your position, survival becomes difficult in this country. In addition, Honourable, it is a good opportunity to make a tidy half-million dollars. Think of what that kind of money can do for you. So, my brother, even though you don't belong to our party, I advise that you support this Bill. In fact, your bag of money is in my office across the lawn. Once you sign for the Bill, you can go home with the money."

As the Governor spoke, the quiet whirring of the recorder in my wristwatch reassured me that the conversation was being recorded.

I thanked the Governor for his candour and compliments but regretted that I would not be able to support the Tenure Prolongation Bill. "As you know, Your Excellency, I belong to a political party that has taken a position to reject the Bill. And as a good party man, it is my duty to obey my party's directives."

"I know, Honourable – but you can always decamp; we are the largest political party in Africa and we will take good care of you."

I laughed, took another spoon of *kunu* and said, "I can't

leave the Labour Party, that is where my constituents belong and …"

"OK, Honourable, let's make this brief; I can double the offer. I am ready to give you a million dollars. What about that?"

# CHAPTER 23

It was late in the evening and Kampala was at her lovely best. The night was dark and beautiful as the evening lights danced and glinted from the distant hills. From my vantage point at the residence of the Nigerian Deputy High Commissioner on Kololo Hill in the Nakasero area of Kampala, it was easy to see why Uganda is called the 'Pearl of Africa'. According to history, it was Winston Churchill who gave Uganda the nickname upon his visit to the country in 1908. Amazed by the country's beauty, Churchill observed that "for magnificent variety of form and colour, profusion of brilliant life – plant, bird, insect, reptile – best for vast scale, Uganda is truly the Pearl of Africa."

Kampala is an interesting place when viewed from its hills as I did that July evening from Kololo. Not many cities could rival the picturesque outlook of Kampala at night. Even in daytime, the city still maintained its beauty. This is unlike some cities, whose flaws are hidden by the bright lights of the night only to be exposed at dawn.

I had gone to Uganda to attend the meeting of the African Peer Review Mechanism organised by the African Union at the Grand Imperial Hotel on Nile Avenue. With me were the leader of our group, Hon. Kalkulus, and Hon. Effiong. Our plan, as discussed earlier in our group, was to use the opportunity of the conference, attended by many African leaders, to present our case against the third-term agenda. In order to look after the interests of the group back home, we had asked Honourables Socrates, Chuks, Yellow, Angel and Lizzy to take charge. As our aircraft prepared to land at Entebbe Airport, one could see pockets of small islands that dotted Lake Victoria.

Looking at Uganda from above, there seemed to be almost as many hills around us as plains. But it was the airport's striking location beside Lake Victoria that gave the town some of its unique qualities, which included several tourist attractions such as Entebbe Wild Life Educational Centre, which showcases several Uganda fauna, particularly chimpanzees and birds. Also in the town are leisure beaches like Entebbe Resort Beach, as well as the Garuga Golf course.

Entebbe, the gateway into Uganda, is situated on Lake Victoria at about 3,800 feet above sea level. The airport is famous for the Israeli commando raid which freed some Israeli athletes held hostage by Arab terrorists several years ago.

The airport, though modern, is a very small one, comparable to Ibadan or Enugu airports. On the Sunday morning when our Ethiopian aircraft landed from Addis Ababa, all was quiet and sedate. As we drove out of Entebbe to Kampala, one could see the wide expanse of Lake Victoria on the right-hand side. Lake Victoria, we were told is the source of the River Nile, whose origin is Jinja, a town 80 kilometres from Kampala.

A drive round Kampala will attest to the fact that despite its relatively poor economy, Uganda is a well –managed place. With a population of about 35 million people with about 2 to 3 million in Kampala alone, the country has been able to provide adequate basic amenities for its people.

The country's regular water and electricity suppliers are sourced from the hydroelectric dam at Jinja. So successful is this dam that Uganda has been able to supply electricity to Kenya and Rwanda as well.

From Kampala Road, the main artery of Kampala, one is able to make forays into other areas of the city, from the upmarket Kololo Hill to Ntinda village, which caters for low-income earners. From here, we ventured to the Mandela Stadium with a capacity for 40,000 spectators, Mulago Hospital, the Bahai temple in the Kanyanyan area of the city as well as the National Theatre and the National Museum. The palace of the Kabaka, the one-time King of Buganda, at Mengo was another interesting tourist attraction. History has it that the king, who was deposed by President Obote, was the actual owner of most of the lands in Kampala. It was the king who, in turn, sold off most parts of the city to their present owners. According to our tourist guide, a road used to lead directly from the palace to the Kabaka's parliament, next to the Supreme Court. It was here that the king used to address his people. Although the walled palace has lost most of its previous glamour, judging from the large human traffic round the place, it was obvious that the current king, who was the son of the old king, still commanded respect in Uganda. As our tourist guide observed, "Even though the king no longer addresses the people, it is believed that they still listen to him even more than they do to the president."

The meeting was well attended by many African Presidents, including some foreign experts, especially those from the Development Partners who were the actual owners of the Peer Review Mechanism.

Not surprisingly, in view of the impending Tenure Prolongation Bill, the Nigerian President could not attend. To represent him came Vice-President Davou Pam, who characteristically did not utter a single word throughout the opening ceremony.

The ceremony over, our friends arranged a meeting between us and the foreign affairs ministers from South Africa, Ghana, Liberia, Uganda and Kenya, countries to which President Oneya had earlier sent emissaries to stress the need for them to support his Tenure Prolongation Bill. Hon. Kalkulus, who spoke on behalf of our group, gave a beautiful ten-page presentation which we had all edited together the previous day.

## WHY WE OPPOSE A THIRD TERM

*Nigeria recently opened another chapter in its political history when the present civilian administration of Chief Ambrose Oneya was sworn in. Naturally, Nigerians at home and in the diaspora expected certain minimum benefits from the civilian administration. These include, among other things, uninterrupted power generation and supply, improved and accessible healthcare system, significant reduction in unemployment, regular payment of pension benefits, improved infrastructure, security of lives and properties, access to sound education and improvement in the general well-being of the citizens.*

*Regrettably, seven years later, these expectations are far from being met. Corruption remains entrenched and endemic. The roads are impassable and with the spate of air crashes, air travel offers no alternative. The railway, which was only comatose before this new government came into power, is now certified dead. Education has been priced out of the reach of the masses. Public education institutions including the universities have never suffered a more terrible fate and neglect. Public health system has collapsed.*

*Rather than create more jobs, this administration derives inexplicable joy from mass termination of employment. On top of all these, the government rewards the patience of the masses with hikes in the prices of petroleum products, which, in turn, ensures that inflation makes nonsense of life and living in Nigeria.*

*This is why it is quite surprising to millions of our people that some people are openly encouraging the President to amend the Constitution and prolong his tenure to enable him to continue with his demonstrated gross incompetence and intolerance.*

## A THIRD TERM IS IMMORAL AND UNCONSTITUTIONAL

*Nigerians are civilised people. It is uncivilised to change the rules of any game in the middle. It is immoral for the President and the government who were sworn in under the 1999 Constitution to seek to retain their offices in clear breach of sections 137(1)b and*

182(1)b of the same Constitution, which unambiguously provide that they cannot seek election into the same offices if they have been "elected to such office at any two previous elections". Even if this government had met all the development needs of the people of Nigeria, which unfortunately is not the case, the third-term agenda would still have been immoral and unacceptable.

*A THIRD TERM WILL LEAD TO INSTABILITY*
To support the third-term agenda is to support political uncertainty and instability. If the proponents succeed, there can be no guarantee that they will not ask for a fourth term or even seek to make Chief Ambrose Oneya life President. This is not far fetched, as the same set of shameless sycophants behind the campaign used similar worn arguments in support of the failed attempts by Babangida and the late Abacha to perpetuate themselves in office. We cannot afford to set a dangerous precedent for other vain leaders who might be tempted to extend their tenure through dubious and fraudulent constitutional amendments. The third-term agenda is a virus that must be resisted.

*A THIRD TERM IS AN INSULT TO NIGERIANS*
Since third-term advocates cannot point to any solid achievement of this government, their strongest argument is that Chief Ambrose Oneya is the only one who can ensure peace and stability in the country. Of course, this is false in all material particulars. General Abacha died several years ago and yet Nigeria has not gone to pieces. As Chief Ambrose Oneya was not born in Aso Rock or as Nigeria's President, it follows that Nigeria will also outlive him. If that is the case, then it is an insult to us as a people to suggest that unless President Oneya remains in office in perpetuity, Nigeria will break up. A country that boasts world-famous scientists, laureates, world-class jurists and notable sportspersons should not be so lightly insulted. The plain truth is that Nigeria will move on with ot without President Oneya.

## A THIRD TERM IS EVIDENCE OF FAILURE

There is a sense in which this 'Oneya or no one else' campaign shows that the President has failed in a significant respect, namely that of grooming a worthy successor who would be acceptable to the electorate. A President who serves for eight years and says he cannot find a trustworthy person to hand over power to is simply saying that he has either monopolised power or has failed totally.

Whichever may be the case, it is clear that the supporters of the third-term agenda do not love Chief Oneya; and if they support the agenda, they do not love themselves. There are millions of Nigerians who are better equipped and have a better temperament than the current President to govern this beloved country of ours.

## A THIRD TERM PROMOTES A CULTURE OF INTIMIDATION AND CORRUPTION

If reports in the media are to be believed, some corrupt governors and other state officials are being forced to support the third-term agenda under threat of prosecution by the EFCC, while those of them who are perceived as clean are being encouraged to fall into line, as they would also benefit from the agenda. However one looks at it, this is nothing but intimidation and gross corruption. Nothing stops state officials from looking at public treasuries when they know they enjoy immunity from prosecution not under the law but if they queue under the third-term umbrella.

It is shameful, to say the least, to use government agencies to intimidate serving public officials or any person for that matter in order to achieve an unconstitutional end. What sort of desperation would make friends of a government that seeks to leave a legacy of waging war against corruption to use corrupt means to make their man remain permanently in office?

## A THIRD TERM IS NOT DIVINELY ORDAINED

Those who claim that President Oneya is the only one that can guarantee unity must be embarrassed, if they have any conscience, concerning how that issue of a third term has badly divided our *people. How united would Nigeria then be under a real third – term presidency of Chief Oneya? There can be no doubt that the country will be fractured. If the president truly believes in the unity of the country, he will not dare attempt a manipulation of the political process to achieve a patently immoral amendment of the Constitution in his favour.*

After the presentation, we spent another two hours answering questions from the diplomats, who seemed very happy with our position, which they believed had cleared many grey areas in the ongoing debate. They therefore promised to finally brief their respective governments on their return home. Afterwards, we interacted with members of the international community present at the meeting. Apart from distributing the prepared handbills, we also tried to update them on the raging controversy. We spent most of the following day sightseeing in preparation for returning to Nigeria later in the day.

A visit to the Uganda parliamentary building, which was built in 1960 by the British before the country's independence in 1962, showed a great legacy of the British colonial rule. Apart from the parliament's dark green seats, the 300 members of parliaments always stood to make their points just like British MPs. Although the country practises the parliamentary system of government, non-party politics is the rule in the country. Candidates are elected on behalf of movements that represent different interest groups. The advantage of this arrangement is that it cuts off the vice-like grip of party barons on the candidates. In a country like Nigeria, where party control of politicians has caused so much anguish, the Ugandan, experiment is worth looking into. The disadvantage of the system is that it gives candidates too much latitude to do whatever they wish with little or no control.

A drive round Kampala will attest to the fact that Uganda has many things in common with Nigeria. Apart from the terrible traffic jams in Kampala, the central part of the city, just as in Lagos, is very congested and dirty. As in Nigeria, motorcycles (called *bodaboda*) very similar to our own *okadas* could be seen all over the place conveying passengers. And just like our own *okadas*, the *bodaboda* have become a menace in the city of Kampala. According to our taxi driver, the motorcyclists are very unruly since many of them do not know how to drive. They only took to the trade due to joblessness. Somehow, Ugandan law protects the *bodaboda* because if you mistakenly knock one of them down, you will pay a fine of five million shillings.

Even though Uganda is similar to Nigeria in many ways, the landlocked nature of the country as well as the poor economy is not all that attractive to Nigerians. As Nigeria's acting High Commissioner in Uganda put it, there are only about 500 Nigerians registered in Uganda.

On our last day in Uganda, we decided to try out some local delicacies such as *matoke*, a kind of banana that is boiled and eaten with local soup. We also found *ugali*, a delicacy made from maize, a delight, even though many Ugandans don't like it. As one of our hosts observed, "The food was imported from Zambia but our people consider it fit only for prisoners."

After our sightseeing, we returned to the closing ceremony of the meeting, where we again had useful discussions with foreign diplomats and journalists. From the discussions, it was obvious that our African brothers and sisters were relieved that some degree of resistance was being put against the Tenure Prolongation Bill. As one foreign diplomat put it, "It will be a disaster if Nigeria, which we all look up to, finally succumbs to the lure of self-perpetuating government. We shall therefore do all we can to support your campaign to see that the Bill is roundly defeated."

# CHAPTER 24

Preparations for the debate on the Constitution (Amendment) Bill which had been going on for the past few months reached a feverish stage the week after our visit to Uganda. Originally planned to improve the democratic experience of the country, the Bill suffered largely due to the inclusion of the Tenure Prolongation Bill. The insertion of this single clause became the proverbial finger that touched oil and soiled others.

On the eve of the commencement of the debate, our group visited the Speaker to reassure him of our support during the debate as long as he kept to the rules of the game. We warned him, however, that if for any reason foul means were introduced to secure the passage of the Bill, we were ready to bring down the House. In his reply, Rt. Hon. Yaya reassured us of his co-operation, "I intend to follow the Constitution, no more, no less. I have sworn an oath to do just that. I will do justice no matter what my personal feelings because at the end of the day, I have a date with my Creator. You can therefore rest assured that the rules as provided for in the Constitution will be followed."

For a Bill to pass into law, both Chambers had to consent to the Bill. Therefore, although he was reputed to be highly cerebral and very honest, our group, which also included some Senators, still decided to see Senator Cyril Okon, the Senate President, in order to gain his support in our fight against the Bill.

Just like the Speaker, the Senate President received our group warmly and promised to uphold the democratic procedures established by the Constitution and the norms of equity, transparency and fair play.

As he put it, "We shall follow due process because we want to ensure that Nigeria survives this crisis. Without due process, political conflict easily graduates to political warfare."

When we complained that members of our group who were against the Bill were being harassed and intimidated by other legislators, he quickly warned all Members of the National Assembly of the need to behave.

He said, "We should not become political entrepreneurs who lust after personal gain, but rather delegates and trustees of the people who will preserve democratic governance. Let us remain guided by the highest ideals of legislative democracy. Let us protect democratic procedures no matter where our votes fall. In this circumstance, the process is more important than the results." The Senate President went further quoting US Senator John McCain's book *Why Courage Matters: the Way to a Braver Life,* in which he wrote: "Courage is not the absence of fear, but the capacity for action despite our fear" He urged us to go on and "do our duty to Nigeria with pride and courage".

Buoyed by these reassuring words we went into the debate with full confidence. We were further assured of victory by an independent television station, AZT, which decided to air the proceedings live. This we believed was a master stroke towards the killing of the Bill since most legislators would not have the nerve to publicly go against the will of their constituents. In fact, those legislators who had been compromised rather than openly contradict their constituents decided to abandon the Chamber when it was their turn to speak.

By the third day of the debate, scores were still equal both ways and we were optimistic that we were going to succeed. Still, we continued keeping to our well honed plans. Even though distribution of the dollar bribes from the sponsors of the bill continued uninterrupted, we were still hopeful of success. I got my turn to speak on the fourth day of the debate. Like other Members, I was given five minutes.

After introducing myself, I went straight to the point. "Mr. Speaker, Honourable colleagues, history is replete with examples of great leaders who knew that the job of nation building cannot be completed by a single individual however good that leader might be. They also knew that democracy is nurtured by an orderly and regular change of power through adherence to a term limit. Great leaders such as George Washington, Thomas Jefferson, Nelson Mandela and Julius Nyerere, in spite of their great record while in office, all resisted pressure to prolong their tenure. In fact, Julius Nyerere of Tanzania once advised leaders that: 'It is better for your people to ask you why you are leaving office, rather than when you are leaving office.' Mr. Speaker, it is also on record that some very bad leaders have plunged their countries into unprecedented social and political turmoil by refusing to leave office at the mandated time. Examples are legion – Mobutu Sese Seko, Robert Mugabe and Daniel Arap Moi."

"It is also on record that in the past 46 years in this country, no democratically – elected Nigerian President has successfully handed over power to a democratically elected successor. This is therefore a good opportunity for President Oneya to write his name in the history books. More importantly, Mr. Speaker, a recent poll by an independent researcher, Afro Barometer, found that 8 out of 10 Nigerians are opposed to the third-term agenda. Therefore, honourable colleagues, if we are actually here to serve the electorate rather than serve ourselves, it is mandatory that we accede to the wishes of our people and say No to a third term."

By the following day, the Bill had been defeated by the Senate and later in the afternoon of the same day, the Speaker had no choice but to suspend the debate in the House of Representatives. As the Speaker puts it, "Early this morning, the Senate laid the matter of constitution amendment Bill to rest. In view of that, the Bill is hereby withdrawn from the chamber."

People jubilated and danced on the streets at the news of the death of the highly controversial Bill. Messages of congratulations immediately started pouring into the National Assembly. In the words of Rtd General Aloke, a former military Governor, "I commend the National Assembly for saving this country from crisis. You did well."

Some serving Governors who had opposed the bill also had this to say: "In a special way, we commend the Members of the National Assembly who, in the face of persecution, intimidation, harassment, coercion and blackmail, have remained resolute, courageous and committed to the cause of fighting the third-term agenda and its attendant consequences."

The death of the Bill was well celebrated by our group, who held an all-night thrash at the Abuja Hilton. It was an exhilarating moment for us all and for the first time in several months I slept soundly.

\* \* \*

The first person I called to inform about our success was Batejo. Like me, she was very happy. "Now that is all over, we can now conclude our wedding arrangements," I said enthusiatically to her on the phone, much to her joy.

The following day, I set out to Kaduna to officially inform my people of the forthcoming wedding and to get everything ready.

From Kaduna, I travelled to Jos to see Batejo's Uncle Tattari, who assured me of his support. "The first thing you have to do is the conversion to Islam. Once that is done, I can then arrange a meeting between you and Batejo's immediate family."

"Can I do the conversion in Kaduna or do I still need to go to Nabordo for this?" I asked.

"I think it's better to have it in Nabordo so that Batejo's relatives can witness it," he replied.

When I arrived in Kaduna and informed my brother James

of my decision to convert to Islam in order to marry Batejo, he was distressed.

"As for me, I have nothing against it," James said," My problem is our mother; you know she is a Deaconess in her church and people look up to her for direction."

"I will explain to her," I said.

"I don't think she will understand. Why don't you and the girl forget this conversion and just practise your different religions? Mama will not be happy, especially now that she's very old. She may lose face in her church."

"Batejo's family had made it clear that I can only be allowed to marry her if I convert. Maybe I shouldn't tell mama. I will just go on with the wedding," I said.

"How's that possible, Sam? It means that you can't invite her to the wedding because once she gets there she will know that you have converted."

"If she will oppose my marrying Batejo then I won't tell her, because I just have to marry the girl."

"No don't do that, Sam. How can you get married without telling your mother? You know how much she loves and trusts you. Why don't we go together and inform her?"

"Before or after the conversion?"

"Of course before. Let her tell you her mind and then from there, you will know what to do."

So, it was then that James and I went to our village to inform my mother of what I was about to do.

Initially, when my mother heard that I was set to remarry she broke into a song of happiness as she praised God for his mercies.

However, when she inquired about the lady and I told her she was a Muslim and that I will need to convert to Islam to marry her, her face suddenly changed.

"Never my son, never. She is the one who has to change to a Christian. You change to a Muslim? No, never, it is not possible!"

"But mama, that is their custom, she is a Fulani Muslim and she won't marry me if I don't convert to Islam."

"Then leave her. Is she the only woman in the world? If she truly loves you, she will change to a Christian and marry you."

There was a moment's quiet in the room as we were all engrossed with our thoughts.

Mama got up, rummaged under her pillow and took out her Bible. "See here: 2 Corinthians 6:14. It says 'Do not be unequally yoked with unbelievers.' That's what the Bible says. It's a pity your father is not alive. I am sure you won't have tried what you are trying ... how do I explain to my church that I, a Deaconess, can allow my son to convert to Islam ..."

"Mama, why are you talking like this? At least we have friends and relatives who are Muslims and they have been good to us," I said.

"That's a different thing, my son. Having Muslim friends and relatives is one thing; marrying them is another. Do you know that it is not good to pollute your blood with that of an unbeliever?" Mama replied as she frantically turned the pages of the Bible in search of a reference with which to back what she has just said.

Seeing that we were not making any progress with mama, I quickly changed the topic. After staying with her for another one hour, we took our leave.

"So, what are you going to do now?" James asked as we later drove back to Kaduna.

I shook my head. "I don't know, I may just go on with the marriage without her."

"Ha, ha, that will not be too good. Why don't you ask Uncle Ishaya to talk to her? As her younger brother, he may be able to convince her."

On getting to Kaduna, we both went to Uncle Ishaya's house and informed him about the problem. Although a Christian, Uncle Ishaya was not as conservative as mama. He promised to see if he could change her mind.

"I am not promising anything, but I will do my best," he said.

As I was about to leave his house, he said, "Conversion is the least of your problems. Have you thought of how to survive the flogging ceremony?"

He was still laughing when I closed the door after him.

\* \* \*

The Speaker of the Federal House of Representatives, Rt. Hon. Yaya Suleiman, was again in a fix. Just when he thought he had seen the last of the crisis in the parliament, another one, this time a gigantic one, had suddenly reared its head. Deep in thought, he kept pacing round his private office as he thought of the way out. When a few hours ago his principal secretary had informed him that the visit of the leadership of the Arewa, the Northern Nigerian Group, was next on his programme for the day, the Speaker was looking forward to a warm interaction with his people. With the demise of the Third – Term Bill, which the Arewa had seriously opposed, the Speaker thought that the visit was to congratulate him on a job well done. He however got the shock of his life when the leader of the delegation, Ambassador Shehu Dalhatu, who was also the Chairman of the Arewa, informed him of Arewa's displeasure over his role in the recently rejected Constitutional Amendment Bill.

As Dalhatu put it, "When everybody from the North was fighting against the tenure prolongation plan, we have evidence to show how you hobnobbed with the President to get the Bill through. In fact, if the Senate had not thrown out the Bill before the House aborted it, it is very unlikely that you could have stopped it. With the failure of the Bill, we have it on good authority that the President wants to punish some top political leaders and businessmen in the country whom he blames for blocking his Bill. Of course, many of these people are from the

North. In order to forestall this move, the Arewa Forum, in collaboration with other political and business leaders in the country, have agreed with the Honourable Members to start impeachment proceedings against Mr. President. We have more than enough charges to get rid of him. We are not here to ask you for any special favour in our impeachment plan. All we ask for is for you to do your duty and not connive with the President. Once you play your role you have no problem. However, failure to do so may force us to move against you."

As the Speaker recollected Alhaji Dalhutu's words, his heart suddenly sank. He knew that an impeachment threat against the President was a serious move which he might not be able to stop. Just then his hotline rang. It was the Senate President.

"Hon. Speaker, I hope the Arewa People have reached you."

"Yes, your Excellency," the Speaker replied.

"We have no choice but to allow the impeachment to go on. The man has overreached himself and there is nothing we can do to help him. Can we meet tonight?"

After fixing an appointment for eight that evening, the Speaker resumed his solitary thoughts. And as he normally did when under stress, he took out his favourite *Gitanjali* from a nearby bookshelf, leafed through and selected another poem."

**Mother, I Shall Weave A Chain**
*Mother, I shall weave a chain of pearls*
*For thy neck with my tears of sorrow.*
*The stars have wrought their anklets*
*Of light to deck thy feet, but*
*Mine will hang upon thy breast.*
*Wealth and fame come from thee*
*And it is for thee to give or to withhold them.*
*But this my sorrow is absolutely mine own,*
*And when I bring it to thee as my offering*
*Thou rewardest me with thy grace.*

Yaya Suleiman went on to read a few more poems. And as he drank them in, they soothed his aching heart and loosened his stiff joints, bringing solace to the gloom around him. As he continued pacing around the room, his Principal Secretary came in to announce the presence of the Deputy Speaker and the other House Leaders in the outer office. The Speaker was reminded that he had fixed a meeting for six in the evening.

"My dear colleagues, I have called you for us to brainstorm on this new crisis before us. To me, it appears to be the biggest challenge of our tenure. This is because some very powerful forces are behind this latest impeachment move. Just a few minutes ago, I got a call from the Senate President on the same issue. He appeared to have made up his mind that they will allow the impeachment to go on. While I am not insisting that Mr. President is innocent of the charges assembled against him, I feel that we should do all we can to soften whatever is done, because I believe that any damage to the President is equally damage to this democracy. This is why I called you for this brief meeting and I will be grateful for your thoughts. By the way, has everybody seen the charges?"

His colleagues shook their heads.

"The charges were brought in today," the Speaker said as he glanced at a heap of documents on his table and brought out some papers which he passed to his colleagues.

"As you can see, there are ten charges against him, even though a few of them may not be strong enough for impeachment. Nevertheless, one strong impeachment offence is enough to get the President out of office."

As the Members went over the charges, the House leader, a former school principal who still had a flair for details and thoroughness, spoke up.

"Hon. Speaker, my colleagues. I want to join the Speaker in acknowledging the fact that this is about our greatest challenge since we got to this house two years ago. However, I do not agree with Mr. Speaker that we should in any way do anything to soften whatever blow might be coming to the President. Don't forget that when this issue of tenure prolongation was first mooted, I spoke against it. I knew that the generality of Nigerians were against it but I was overruled. Now, it is this same Bill that has formed the first impeachable charge against the President. I was in the lobby when the Arewa people came. I spoke to a few of them and they are all pointing accusing fingers at Mr. Speaker for having colluded with the President on the Third – Term Bill. In addition, the Senate President has decided to distance himself from this impeachment bid. He wants the law to take its normal course; therefore, Mr. Speaker, we should not be seen to be colluding again with the President. Let's just do our work and leave the final decision to the House."

After the leader, the other principal officers spoke in the same vein, all advocating that the Speaker should not intervene but allow the law to take its course.

Predictably, it was only the Deputy Speaker who did not speak since he did not want to be seen to be openly criticising his immediate boss; rather, he asked: "When will the impeachment bid be tabled?"

"On Tuesday, in five days' time," the Speaker said as the meeting continued.

# CHAPTER
# 25

I converted to Islam on the day I turned thirty-five. It was a dull overcast day in July. It had threatened to rain throughout my four-hour trip from Abuja, but not a drop fell. I enjoyed the beautiful scenery from Abuja, especially the jagged hills and sharp valleys between Jos and Bauchi. Once in a while, as my car hurtled down sharp ravines, I had the eerie feeling of being buried by the huge mountains.

By midday, when I entered the mosque in Nabordo, the sky was clear of all cloud. Even though scores of Batejo's relatives whom I had invited for the occasion were in joyous mood, delighted that I had taken the most important step in my preparations to wed their daughter, the same could not be said for my own relatives, who had refused to come with me to the mosque. Since my Uncle Ishaya could not persuade my mother to give her blessing for my conversion, the old woman had instructed my other relatives to stay away from the event.

"Can you imagine a whole man changing his religion just because of a small girl?" My mother told anyone who cared to listen, "Is it not the woman who should convert to Christianity? Only God knows the kind of Fulani charm they had used on the poor boy."

It was only my brother James and Uncle Ishaya who, more out of pity than conviction, decided to follow me. Two of my colleagues in the National Assembly who were Muslims, Hon. Baba Mohammed and Hon. Taju Rasaki, also accompanied me.

Dressed in a bright white *galabiya* and a skullcap, I entered the mosque clutching my newly acquired Koran under my left armpit while a brand new tasbihu dangled from my right hand.

The Imam, a short thickset man who alternated between Hausa and Fulfulde in his sermon, asked me to recite my conversion:

"I believe in one God, Supreme and Eternal,
Infinite and Mighty, Merciful and Compassionate,
Creator and Provider who does not have a son, daughter or father. I also believe that Mohammed is his only messenger."

The Imam later reminded me of the need to pray five times a day and be ready to undertake all the expected fasting that a Muslim is supposed to undertake.

After I had taken the name Mahmud which Batejo had said was her grandfather's, the Imam rounded off the short ceremony with the prayer.

In the name of God, Most Gracious, Most Merciful: Praise be to God, the cherisher and sustainer of the worlds; most gracious, most merciful, master of the day of judgment. You do we worship, and your aid do we seek. Show us the straight way, the way of those on whom you have bestowed your grace, those whose portion is not wrath, and who go not astray.

After the ceremony, we all moved to Uncle Tatari's house for some refreshment. As the drinks and refreshments were served, I went up to Uncle Tatari. After thanking him for his assistance, I enquired about the next steps.

"The next thing is the traditional flogging ceremony which we call *Sharo*." When he saw the expression on my face he added, "I thought Batejo had told you?"

"Yes she mentioned it, but I thought it was all a joke, especially after those thugs had almost killed me the other day."

"Ha ha ha, that one was not a ceremony. It was an unfortunate incident. The *Sharo* is mandatory and you have to go through it."

The thought of being flogged with those menacing Fulani sticks was not palatable to me and I was momentarily disturbed; still I tried to put up a bold face.

"When will this be?" I asked.

"We normally have it twice a year, during the dry season harvest and secondly during *Id-el-kabir,* meaning that the next one is next month. I also hope that you are aware that the contest is between you and Gidado."

"Gidado? Why? I thought you promised to return his cows."

"The boy has insisted on competing for the hand of Batejo; so both of you will come for the ceremony and whoever is braver will marry Batejo."

"Sorry Uncle Tatari, I ... I ... don't understand," I said as panic came over me, "I thought that all I need to do is convert to Islam and pay for the cows. I never knew I had to compete with Gidado again. So, in case the boy wins the flogging competition, what happens to all the money I have spent, not to mention my conversion to Islam?"

Tatari broke into loud, raucous laughter, "Why are you contemplating failure? Are you not a man? If you seriously want Batejo, then you should work for her hand in marriage. You shouldn't allow any small issue to distract you. We have our methods of getting rid of those we don't want and getting those we do. Don't worry, Mahmud, I know how much you want Batejo and I will help you to realise your dreams. Just trust me."

\* \* \*

With the threat of impeachment hanging on his neck like an albatross, President Ambrose Oneya GCFR, President and Commander-in-Chief of the Nigerian Armed Forces, knew that he was fighting perhaps the most important battle of his political life. In his early sixties, Oneya controlled the political machine of the largest party in Africa with a combination of favours and a generous lacing of threats. He knew the dirty secrets of most of his political allies and adversaries through his well organised security and secret police networks.

His antics in suppressing the opposition and adversaries were a throwback to the Second Republic, where the grand auction of principle and political intrigue were the order of the day. His personal life was no better as he found it difficult to resist a quarrel, a drink or a pretty woman ... even at this, Oneya had no apologies to make. As he once put it, "Politics is not a gentleman's game and Nigerians need to be rescued from the vicious grips of a maniac that has long held them hostage. As long as I am able to do this, I have no regrets for my action."

The President's enigmatic character breathed through every word. He spoke, revealing a character as one simple, humble, innocent and capable of deception or intrigue; yet also a character larger than life, boisterous, combative and occasionally disingenuous. It was his Machiavellian attitude of the end justifying the means that had made his critics very wary of him.

President Oneya came across to many like a man of action, a soldier of fortune living for adventure, loving the fight more than the cause, straddling the country like a conqueror, not inclined to give much room for his opponents or the opinions of critics. Despite all these negative traits, the President was eager to reassure whoever cared about his genuine love for Nigeria. As he always put it, "I may have a caustic tongue but not itching fingers. If anybody can prove that I have stolen a kobo of Nigerian's money, I am ready to resign from office immediately."

Niger Delta man that he was, Ambrose Oneya loved his drink. He wasn't the first Head of State to be so. Thatcher loved her whisky, while Churchill claimed to have drunk half a bottle of champagne for lunch everyday of his adult life, declaring that he took more out of alcohol than alcohol ever took out of him. The same can be said of Ambrose Oneya.

From his wide security network, Oneya had got wind of

the ever-tightening political vice round his throat. While he knew he could never bank on the Senate President's support, he had thought that the Speaker would help him in the House of Representatives. However, with the subtle threat from the Arewa Council to the Speaker, Oneya now realised that he would need all the luck in the world to stay afloat.

Glancing up from the file he was reading, President Oneya pressed a button under his table as his Principal Secretary answered.

"Please ask the VP, the SSG and Senate Smollet to meet me in the private room."

Thereafter, he placed calls to the Deputy Speaker and the Deputy Senate President, the only remaining allies he could boast of in the National Assembly.

About half an hour later, the President was in his private office with his kitchen cabinet. He did not waste time as he quickly laid the issue on his mind squarely before the gathering.

"Gentlemen, in a few days' time, a motion for my impeachment will commence simultaneously before the Senate and the House of Representatives. I have seen the charges, ten in all, ranging from my alleged attempt to illegally extend my tenure to non-compliance with budgets passed by the National Assembly and sundry other matters. As you are all aware, impeachment in Nigeria is a purely political issue. This is because the Constitution allows it. Let me just refresh your mind on what the Constitution says." He stretched forward for a copy of the Nigerian Constitution on his table,

*Section 143 of the Constitution under the caption Removal of President from Office states that the President or Vice-President may be removed from office whenever a notice of any allegation in writing signed by not less than one-third of the Members of the National Assembly is presented to the President of the Senate stating that the President or Vice-President is guilty of gross misconduct in the performance of the functions of his office, detailed particulars of which shall be specified.*

President Oneya marked the page and put away the Constitution.

"As of yesterday, this first requirement has already been met, since the required number of the Members of the National Assembly have already signed the motion. It is also obvious that with the current positions of the Senate President and the Speaker, my impeachment is almost a fait accompli. I have therefore summoned you all to hear your views on the way forward."

The Vice-President was the first to speak, "Mr. President, we are all politicians and we know that it is never over until it's over. My advice therefore is for us to fight this matter to the last. Democracy, they say, is a game of numbers. While it is true that one-third of the Members of the National Assembly should sign the notice of impeachment, section 143 subsection 9 states that 'the final decision must be taken by not less than two-thirds majority of each House of the National Assembly.' Mr. President, if we move quickly, we can make sure that the two-thirds majority is not achieved."

"How do you want to do this? Oneya asked.

"Ha, Mr. President, the same way we have been doing it ... Senator Smollet is our man in the National Assembly, he knows their language. All they want is fertilizer, or whatever they call it. If it needs emptying all our 5-billion-dollar foreign reserve, I think we should do it."

There was silence in the room as each person became lost in thought. Then the SSG raised his hand.

"Yes, Mr. Secretary?" the President said.

"Sir, pardon my naïvety, but I want to know what the Constitution means by "gross misconduct" and whether we can challenge this in a court of law."

The Deputy Senate President answered

"*Section 143 subsection 11 of the Constitution defines gross misconduct as a grave violation or breach of the provisions of the Constitution or a misconduct of such nature as amounts in the opin-*

*ion of the National Assembly to gross misconduct*. From this, it is obvious that it is difficult to escape from the grip of the National Assembly when it comes to the issue of gross misconduct since the law has given them this latitude to decide this.

"On the issue of going to court, subsection 10 of Section 143 states that: *No proceedings or determination of the panel or of the National Assembly or any matter relating thereto shall be entertained or questioned in any court.* This again goes to show that Mr. President cannot use the court to stop the proceedings.

Your Excellency, if you permit, can I make my own contribution to the matter?"

The President nodded.

"As the VP said earlier, democracy is a game of numbers. It is also important to note Mr. President's observation that impeachment is always political. Once the system (which in this case is the National Assembly) has decided to get rid of the President, it is difficult to stop the procedure. The VP spoke of spending money; from my experience from the recently botched Constitution Review Bill, money has its limits. Over 3.5 billion naira was spent, yet we didn't get what we wanted. The legislators will definitely take the money but will refuse to do the President's will. Furthermore, if care is not taken, the decision to use money may even be used against the President as another impeachment offence. More important, Your Excellency, is for us to understand the full motive behind the impeachment plan. What is being planned is actually to fully humiliate Mr. President by hauling him before the courts after the impeachment exercise. My advice therefore is to for us to abort the whole process of impeachment even before it takes off."

"How do we do this?" President Oneya asked.

"Well, Your Excellency, it's hard for me to say; but the best option in the whole scenario is resignation."

"No, no! Resignation for what?" the VP shouted, trying very hard not to be seen to support an act that would directly favour him.

"I also disagree that the President should resign," Senator Smollet said. "As the VP suggested, we can fight this through; all we need is to assemble the right legislators and adequately empower them. We can also appeal to public opinion."

"Which public opinion? With due respect to the President, current public opinion, especially coming after the demise of the Tenure Prolongation Bill, is very much against us. It will only worsen matters if we seek public opinion" the Deputy Speaker said.

For the next two hours, the arguments for and against the President's resignation went up and down like the temperature chart of a serious illness.

\* \* \*

I thought I was dreaming; but when the incessant ringing of the doorbell persisted, I woke to realise that the noise was real. A peep through my bedroom window showed the sight of a familiar figure on my doorstep.

"Yes, who is it?" I asked.

"Honourable, it's me, Senator Smollet."

With a frown, I took a look at the bedside clock, it was two in the morning.

Pulling on my house coat, I went downstairs to open the door.

I had never seen Senator Smollet looking so terrible before. Always spare and balding, he had now visibly shrunk as if recovering from a debilitating illness.

"Yes Senator, please come in, what is the matter?"

Senator Smollet apologised for waking me up and flopped tiredly into the sofa. Then with red eyes and husky voice, he told me his mission. "You must be aware of the motion of impeachment hanging over the President."

When I nodded, he said, "I have just finished a marathon meeting at the Presidency and the decision was taken to save the

President at all costs. In view of your expertise in parliamentary crisis you were pointed out as one of the likely spearheads of the move to save the President."

"Me? A Member of the opposition to save the President? What about all the leaders of the so-called largest party in Africa?"

"Yes, Honourable, you are reputed to stand on principles and very honest to boot. And, although this is a personal issue, your Bill which is about to be signed by the President may be adversely affected if the President is forced out."

Suddenly, Smollet's mission began to make sense. It was subtle blackmail. Knowing how committed I was to the Bill, it would be believed that I would be ready to do all I could to make sure that it was signed into law before Mr. President left office.

Sensing my change of countenance, Smollet said: "Like I said, the issue of the Bill is a secondary matter. It is your beliefs in due process and the rule of law that made the President decide on you."

"But Senator, the impeachment charges look fair to me. Honestly, I can't fault them."

"I know, Honourable Bakura, but this is Nigeria. Agreed, the man made a political miscalculation; does that equate to impeachment? If politicians in this country are to be punished for every offence they commit, I doubt if any one of us can go scot free. In addition, most of the charges against the President were decisions taken collectively by other members of the party. It is therefore against the rule of law to punish just the President alone for the sins of others."

"That's why he is the President. He has to take responsibility for whatever goes wrong in his government. Talking seriously, Senator, from all indications, it's as if the legislators, especially those from your party, have made up their mind to sacrifice the President. Even the Arewa Council, which was expected to defend him in a situation like this, are active sponsors of the impeachment. It therefore looks to me like a bad case."

"Well, Honourable, you have a point there; but we all know that in politics it's not over until it's over. We can't just fold our arms and do nothing."

He dipped his hand into the pocket of his kaftan and brought out a large envelope which he extended to me.

"This is 200,000 dollars, it's just for take-off … one million dollars will be yours if you can pull this off, while Members will take 200,000 each. Some extra money will be paid for logistics."

I flinched away from his outstretched hand.

"No Senator, I won't take the money. Not that I don't like money, but because I want to be sure I can deliver first. Just give me a few days to investigate. If in truth the President has a good case, I will take it up; but if not, I wouldn't touch it for all the dollars in the World Bank."

# CHAPTER

# 26

Lizzy shouted angrily, stabbing her finger in my face, "I can't believe that you would do such a stupid thing. How can you change your faith because of a girl and on top of it subject yourself to a demeaning and degrading custom of a public flogging ceremony, all in the name of love?"

I had just woken up after Senator Smollet's early morning visit when the doorbell rang again. After a welcome hug, she had clung to me, her mouth pouted in readiness for a kiss. It was my perfunctory kiss on the cheek that infuriated her and forced me to tell her about my forthcoming wedding to Batejo.

Although Lizzy was as usual enchanting, in a body-hugging red dress that accentuated her youthful curves, I was resolute in my determination to marry Batejo. Disappointed, she rolled out of my arms and turned away from me so that I could no longer see her face. I could sense her bewilderment and pain but there was no way I could help her. At least my conscience was clear, having given her enough chance at the outset of the relationship. I was still trying to figure out how to handle the situation when Lizzy turned round and looked at me directly in the face, "Look Sam, em … em …" She was having tremendous difficulty finding the right words. "I am fond of you, very fond, you know that. I am sorry I was a bit hesitant in the beginning. I wasn't sure of your intentions, but now …" She paused for a painful moment. "I need you, Sam, I need a strong reliable man whom I can trust after my failed marriage." Two large tears rolled down her cheeks.

I went over to her and held her head. With my handkerchief, I wiped away her tears. "I am sorry Lizzy, I was also very eager in the beginning. You remember I told you how well suited we could be to each other in view of our shared ethnic background and marital circumstances. Not only did you decline, you went ahead to humiliate me by flaunting your relationship with some of my colleagues. Now that I have found someone very dear to me and I have given my word to her, I cannot back out."

She was still trying hard to keep hold of her emotions as the recollections of what I had said stirred deep within her. At the same time, she desperately wanted to convince me that she had made a great mistake. "But Samuel, I like you very much, I really do and on a serious note, I have a feeling that what you are doing is not right. You changed your faith without your mother's blessings and now you want to subject yourself to a sadistic and barbaric if not dangerous ceremony, all because of a nineteen-year-old girl. Think about this: you are well educated, a Member of Parliament who should be in the forefront of advocacy against early marriage and obsolete customs and traditions, only to be part of it. And don't forget that you will be contesting this flogging ceremony with boys who are far younger and more physically fit than you. Many of those boys, for your information, will have fortified themselves with herbal medicine and charms that will make them resistant to pain. From my investigation, some people have died during such ceremonies due to the severe beating. Now you want to go and endanger your life for nothing."

Lizzy moved closer. "OK, Sam, tell me more about this your Fulani girlfriend."

It was an obvious ploy to waste my time, weaken my resolve and make me change my mind about Batejo. All the same, my tongue was loosened.

"She is nineteen, precisely half my age. And she is, adjectives fail me, a stunning captivating beauty. And point of correction: she is not my girlfriend but my fiancée, my betrothed," I explained.

"And who is your rival?" Lizzy asked.

"You mean my fiancée's ex?" I snarled, "His name is Gidado, an illiterate poverty-stricken cowherd."

"Hmm, you call a Fulani with lots of cows poverty stricken? Yes, illiterate he may be but not a poor man. Be careful, Sam, never underestimate your rival, especially if he is a Fulani. By the way, is the girl literate?"

"Oh, yes, her English is as beautiful as her face," I replied. "Now, before this snail, excuse me, this Gidado slowly completes the dowry of eight cows I would have done it all, received my flogging and taken my wife."

In the elation and vanity of the moment, I fished out my wallet and drew out Batejo's photograph. "This," I said with the air of a six-year-old boy displaying his Christmas gift of toy plane, "is my red girl, Batejo."

It was a mistake, a grievous blunder. Lizzy seized the photograph, stared long and hard at it and hissed. "She is a stunner all right," she admitted, "but who wouldn't be – at nineteen! At nineteen, Sam you would have killed to get at my body."

I half-conceded the point. "You still are there, sizzling Lizzy, a sight for sore eyes."

"Sam, you cannot marry this tomato-faced Fulani girl, full stop. I, Elizabeth Kande Bello, will do everything in my power to stop you."

I laughed."Really, Lizzy, what can you do? I love the girl and there is nothing anybody can do to stop me from marrying her. More importantly, I have the assurances of her uncle that nothing bad will happen to me during the ceremony and I will do all …"

Unfortunately, Elizabeth wasn't listening to me anymore as she took her handbag and fled. All I could hear was the clack of her high heels on the pavement outside.

After Lizzy's exit, I got dressed, had breakfast and drove to the Speaker's house. It being a Wednesday, the House would not be sitting until two in the afternoon. I found the Speaker at breakfast with two other Members. Although I was not happy, I joined them at the table, more to listen to their conversation than to eat.

The discussion soon moved to the issue of the president's impeachment.

"It is a very bad case for the President," one of the Members from Adamawa State was saying, "I was at the party headquarters yesterday and everybody was unhappy with the international uproar in the wake of the Tenure Prolongation Bill. They believed that it gave the country a very bad image."

"But I thought that the bill had the party's backing?" I said.

"Not exactly," said the other Member from Sokoto, "We had a lot of division over it within the party but you know our people – since money was involved, they quietly followed the President. However, when the whole thing crashed, everybody ran away and now they are heaping all the blame on the President."

"The most painful thing is that the North believes that the President stabbed them in the back. Having agreed that the North should produce the next President, to have attempted to perpetuate himself in office was a letdown. That's why they can't forgive him and that's why they want to get him out," the Member from Adamawa added.

"And you think they will succeed?" I asked.

"It is not whether I think they will succeed," the Sokoto Member said. "They have already succeeded. Once the motion is tabled next Tuesday, the Chief Justice will announce the names of the seven-person panel that we have already selected."

"But according to the Constitution, the panel has three months to report to both houses and ..." I said, but the Sokoto Member cut in.

"Not three months; what the Constitution says in section 143 subsection 7(b) is '*within* three months'. This can even happen in 48 hours, as long as it's within three months."

The Speaker who had kept quiet throughout the discussion now spoke. "I have already advised the President to resign instead of being thrown out of office in disgrace and later prosecuted."

"Ha, ha Speaker, have you ever heard of a Nigerian political office-holder resigning from office? Even if he was caught red – handed in corruption?"

"But he has no choice but to resign; if he doesn't, its jail straightaway," the Adamawa Member said.

"I heard that the President is fighting back. He keeps holding meetings every day with party chieftains, community leaders and Governors," I said.

"But everyone has been telling him the truth; and still he won't listen. He has even sent his National Assembly liaison officer to go about sharing money," the Sokoto Member said.

"You mean Senator Smollet? That one is a thief. He's only looking for ways of taking care of himself. He won't tell the President the truth," the Adamawa Member said.

Just before we rose from breakfast, I asked the Speaker about the issue of unsigned Bills under the President in the event of his impeachment.

"We have forwarded six Bills to him for signature. What the Constitution says is that if after 120 days, a Bill is not signed into law, the National Assembly can veto the President."

"But we may not have up to 120 days before his departure if he is impeached," I said.

"In that case, the Vice-President who will later become the President can sign the Bills. At least it's the same administration," the Speaker observed.

It was now clear to me that from all indications the President had a very bad case and my Bill would not suffer in the event of his impeachment. Consequently, I could not accept Senator Smollet's offer of working for the President. That same evening, I sent a text message to the Senator to confirm my position.

\* \* \*

The *Sharo* ceremony, as practised by many nomadic Fulani ethnic groups, is a public flogging event which is a test of endurance before a young man can marry. During the ceremony, usually held twice a year in the marketplace, young men who are contesting for the hand of a maiden in marriage are expected to undergo severe flogging in public without flinching.

Since Gidado had refused to withdraw his interest in Batejo, Gidado and I had been paired to each undergo the flogging ceremony to see which of us would have the hand of the young woman in marriage.

"We normally hold the ceremony twice a year. One during the dry season harvest period and the other during the Muslim festival of Id-el-kabir," Uncle Tatari informed me one weekend when I went to see him in Bauchi on his invitation.

"Which of us will be flogged first?" I asked.

"We won't know until the day of the ceremony. Both of you will come prepared, stripped to the waist. We shall draw lots and whoever draws first will be flogged first. The second person will undergo his own flogging during the next ceremony," he said.

"You mean I have to wait another three months or so before I can marry Batejo?" I asked.

"Yes, that's the culture."

So it was that my *Sharo* festival was fixed for the second week of September after the dry season guinea cornharvest. It was a market day and the whole community turned out gaily dressed. It must have been a community of many clans, for the crowd was very large.

There was a lot of drumming, dancing and acrobatic displays. As a prelude to the event, there were dances by the maidens as well as performances by well-known minstrels and tricksters.

As I prepared to leave Uncle Tatari's house where I had stayed before the event, James, my brother, called me aside. "Are you sure you want to go through this? Is it worth it? Those other boys are very young and can withstand serious pain. Are you sure you can handle it? I don't want any terrible thing to happen to you."

"I will be okay. In addition, Uncle Tatari has already given me some herbal medicine which will prevent the pain. He has assured me that I won't feel any pain."

I was accompanied to the open space in the market place by James, Uncle Tatari, my friend Hon. Baba Mohammed, Batejo and some of her relatives.

All in all, we were about ten suitors to be flogged for twenty maidens. I was now naked to the waist, my body rubbed with shea butter mixed with some herbal cream as prepared by Uncle Tatari. On the field were gaily—dressed maidens and drummers who were already performing their acts. Dressed in their traditional hand-woven white native material, the dancers perfomed their acts. While the men used their *sanda and hats,* the ladies used their milk gourds to accentuate their seductive dance steps. The whole place was in a festive mood and as the maidens to be contested for came out to dance, the tempo of the drums increased. Moments later, it was our turn to move to the field. The tempo of the drums now increased as several youths who were asked to accompany us cried shrilly and mumbled some incantations and broke out in songs. Some of the Fulani men, including some of Gidado's friends, openly admired my athletic body and appeared worried that I might eventually win the contest. But it was not all commendation. While some of the youths praised my courage as a non-Fulani in coming out for the flogging ceremony, others sneered at me for daring to come and steal one of their best girls from their midst.

"You will be so flogged that you won't be able to find your way home again," they threatened.

I only smiled and promised to go home with Batejo.

Soon the contest began with the first two contenders drawing lot. The fellow who won the lot was a tall dark fellow who quickly struck a pose, brought out his lipstick and mirror and started applying it while his rival and two other youths prepared to start flogging him.

As the long cane struck his body, blood spurted from the ensuing bruises, but the man did not flinch. Stroke after stroke landed on his body, drawing blood; but the fellow continued applying his lipstick, even asking for more strokes. I couldn't believe it … the man was even re-doing his make-up in the process, admiring his face in the mirror while the maiden he was contesting for came from time to time to wipe the sweat from his face! After the mandatory nine strokes, the boy did not show any sign of pain; he was carried shoulder-high by his relatives and well-wishers, while the maiden being courted helped him to wipe away the sweat and blood from his body.

"He will have the chance to also flog his rival during the next festival," Uncle Tatari explained to me.

"How then do they decide the winner?" I asked.

"The same referees who were here today will judge the contest and decide which of the two men showed more courage," he said.

The next man was not that lucky; either he was too weak or his charms failed him. The fellow could no longer bear the pain and fled from the field after the third stroke of the cane.

Two other young men went for the ceremony and both succeeded before Gidado and I were called out.

Apparently, our case must have become very popular, for the drummers now went into frenzy as the tempo of the drums increased and more youths cried shrilly. The news must have spread, how a non-Fulani wanted to marry one of them.

While Gidado was accompanied by about ten well-wishers, I had only four with me. In a corner I could see Batejo resplendent in her red outfit as she gaily waved to me.

Soon Gidado and I came face to face and I could see that he was a little jittery. This, coupled with the herbal medicine given me by Uncle Tatari, gave me some confidence. We drew lots and, much to my joy, I was the one to be flogged first; Gidado had to wait for his turn the following season.

Three youths including Gidado were to administer the flogging at the rate of three strokes each. Gidado was to administer the last three strokes. As the tempo of the music increased, I struck a pose by crossing my legs as I had been taught by Batejo.

I took the first six strokes without flinching, even laughing and taunting the fellows administering the strokes, despite the fact that by then blood had started oozing out of my chest wounds. Impressed by my performance, the drummers increased the tempo of their drums while Batejo came forward smiling and wiped the sweat and blood from my body. It was now Gidado's turn and I could see his worried and nervous looks as he prepared to flog me. He dipped his forefinger into a small leather pouch by his waist, and brought out a whitish cream with which he smeared the tip of his long cane. I taunted him by gesturing that he should be quick. As the first stroke landed on my back, pain like an electric current ran through my body. Still I managed to appear unruffled. However, as the second stroke landed on my chest, blood spurted out of my body as a searing pain of unimaginable degree overtook me. Instantly, I let out an ear-shattering scream, tried to flee from the field but collapsed in a heap on the dusty ground crying, *wayyo Allah! wayyo Allah!*

Instantly, the Gidado group burst into a frenzy of excitement, screaming and shouting their victory. It was as if the whole community was in a conspiratorial celebration-singing while some of Gidado's able-bodied aides lifted him shoulder-high. From my misty eyes, I saw Batejo where she had collapsed in a corner of the field weeping while Uncle Tatari and James rushed to me cradling my head and pouring cold water on my body. Suddenly, I thought I saw a figure like Lizzy's. It couldn't possibly be, I reckoned. But … was she not? Was she not the one dancing and making frantic effort to be visible? Whao! She jeered at me! What could she have in connection with this episode? As I was held up, I felt my knee-joints melt and my legs gave way.

# CHAPTER 27

The motion for the impeachment of President Ambrose Oneya moved swiftly in each House of the National Assembly. In line with the Constitution, the Chief Justice of the Federation appointed a panel of seven persons who in his opinion were of unquestionable integrity to investigate the allegation against the President.

Even at this stage, the President and his men were still confident that either the panel would rule that the allegation has not been proved or it would be impossible for each House to raise the two-thirds majority to adopt the panel's report.

However, when instead of using the three-month period available to it, the panel turned in its report within three weeks, the President and his men got jittery. Despite all efforts, the contents of the report could not be ascertained. On the day that the panel submitted its report to the Senate President, President Oneya called an emergency meeting of his kitchen cabinet.

As usual, the VP stuck to his earlier suggestion that the President should not give in, "I still believe, Your Excellency, that the panel's report will be favourable. If not, why did it take them just three weeks to reach a verdict when the law allows them up to three months to do so? This is especially when His Excellency was able to successfully debunk most of the allegations during his defence."

Senator Smollet too was very optimistic that the President had successfully scaled the hurdle. "We are reaching out to Members of the National Assembly on a daily basis. As of today, we have been able to settle about 250 members in the House of Representatives as well as over 90 Senators. With this, it is obvious that even if the report of the panel is bad, it will be impossible to get the required two-thirds of Members in each House to adopt the report."

However, both the Deputy Senate President and the Deputy Speaker took a different line.

According to the Deputy Senate President, "Although I am not privy to the contents of the panel's report, the mood of Members in both Houses is not very encouraging. While I don't want to disbelieve Senator Smollet's report, he must know that the fact that Members collected money from you is no guarantee that they will do your will. It happened during the Constitution Amendment Bill; therefore, I don't want us to use that yardstick to gauge Members' voting patterns. In addition, Your Excellency, don't forget that the Constitution stipulates that each House must consider the panel's report within 14 days. From the feelers I am getting from the Speaker and the President, the report will be debated within the next three days and therefore there is no time to lose. Once the report is adopted and the impeachment carried out, anything can happen to the President and this is what we want to avoid. From my discussion with the Speaker, it is possible for the National Assembly to arrange a soft landing for Mr. President."

"What kind of soft landing?" the VP asked.

"I am not sure yet, but I believe that if Mr. President resigns and spares the National Assembly the burden of going through the whole process of the impeachment, he can be given immunity from prosecution after leaving office."

It was now the President's turn to speak.

"I want to thank you all for your support and comments. As you all know, it is not easy to be a political leader anywhere in the world, especially in a developing nation such as ours. I have been in political office in one form or the other for the past 30 years and I believe that on balance I have achieved a lot. Few leaders contribute more than a thread or two to the tapestry of history, but I like to think that mine has been strong, positive, colourful strands of good public service. I believe that I have been able to alter the perceptions of one or two key political issues and exerted a modest amount of both power and influence for the greater good. It would be tedious to itemise these achievements but, looking back on my political life in general, I feel much more fulfillment than disappointment. Even on this current allegation for impeachment, you all know that everything I did was the party's decision. The truth is that in this country, real power in government lies in the hands of three or four people: the Party Chairman, the President, the Chairman of the Board of Trustees of our party, and perhaps a couple of trusted colleagues like you. Nothing I did was not discussed at the highest level of the party. This is why I am surprised that the party has decided to abandon me at this hour of need. I have decided to see the whole thing through. I will not resign and will not ..."

At that point, the President's Principal Secretary, a cousin of the Speaker, entered the room and whispered to the President, who quickly excused himself and followed the PA outside.

A few minutes later, the President was back in room 109, looking terribly disturbed. He again thanked members of the group for coming and quickly brought the meeting to an end.

As soon as the last of his guests left the room, President Oneya called his aides and was escorted back to his residence a few corridors away from his office. He was welcomed home by Beatrice, his wife of thirty years. "How did it go today, my darling? Any news from the impeachment people?" She asked.

"Bad news, my dear."

"What happened?"

"The panel supported the impeachment."

"What? How did you know?"

"The PS told me."

Beatrice, a former student beauty queen, now corpulent in her mid-fifties but still attractive, sat next to her husband at the dining table.

"I'm sorry, dear, so what's next?"

"The National Assembly wants me to resign in exchange for immunity from prosecution; they call it 'soft landing'."

"Softlanding? You didn't do anything that requires prosecution, so why do you need a soft landing? I think you should see this thing through. You are not going to resign. No African or Nigerian President has ever resigned and you shouldn't be the first one. Even Babangida didn't resign. He only stepped aside. We still have a chance to get them, my dear. Cheer up and let me get you your food," Beatrice Oneya said and went to the kitchen.

Alone in his study after dinner, Ambrose Oneya was deep in thought as he went through the events of the day. Left to him, he would have resigned. He didn't want to be at the mercy of those goons who would grill him and take away all he had made during his 30 years in politics. At over 60, he was not particularly looking forward to spending his last years in prison. Better to resign and spend his wealth on the beaches of Bahamas than in the scorching heat of Biu prison in Bornu state. The more he thought of his problems the more he got worked up. "What do they want with me?" He screamed to himself inside his head. "Why are they persecuting me like this?"

At least, they had taken all the decisions together. Alone in the study, he had no one to turn to, no one to share his misery and offer consolation. He was now a lonely figure, a sincere and even devout man who made one mistake – of trying to illegally extend his tenure – and now had to pay for it. He wondered what was wrong in what he had done; after all, many African Presidents at one time or the other had done a similar thing and were now enjoying themselves. He remembered his friend Paul Biya of Cameroun, Robert Mugabe of Zimbabwe, or even Museveni of Uganda; all had extended their stay by hook or crook.

Why then him? He now remembered his mother's Sunday School lesson on the need to pay for one's sins or be consumed by hell fire. He now felt the flames licking at his feet. But it's not fair, he thought. He had worked so hard all these years, deserved so much and yet it had come to this. He knew he had to call it quits. There was no point in going on, only to be humiliated at the end and spend his old age in gaol. Resignation was out of the question. Beatrice would have none of that and he was scared of the prison that he knew certainly awaited him if impeached by the National Assembly.

Suddenly, an idea flashed through his feverish brain. Through tired and misty eyes, he reached into the drawer of his desk, fumbled through the papers there and took out a loaded revolver. It would be good to end it all. He was still thinking of where to put the cold Luger when the door opened and Beatrice entered the study, accompanied by Senator Smollet.

When Beatrice saw the gun, she let out an ear-splitting scream. "Put that thing away!" She shouted.

President Oneya was still trembling when his wife and Smollet reached him. Quickly Beatrice took the gun safely out to the kitchen. Between Beatrice and Smollet, Oneya was persuaded to try one last time to reach the Members of the National Assembly.

"Your Excellency, I have just reached an agreement with the Members of the National Assembly. We have agreed that another thirty million dollars will do the trick," Smollet said, silently smacking his lips.

"Thirty million dollars? Where do you think I can get that kind of money?" Oneya asked.

"But darling, we …" Beatrice began, but her husband's hard stare stopped her.

"Your Excellency, $30 million is nothing compared with losing your position and facing prosecution later," Smollet said.

"Yes darling, it's worth trying. Don't give up so easily, you can call your foreign partners to assist. It's better than being humiliated out of office," said Mrs Oneya.

After a lot of argument, President Oneya agreed to give out twenty million dollars, fifteen to the House of Representatives and five to the Senate, to stave off his impeachment.

The following morning, armed with the money, Senator Smollet arrived in the premises of the National Assembly to deliver the money to his contacts. Senator Julius Kanu collected the money on behalf of the Senators, while Honourable Elizabeth Bello collected on behalf of the Members. Both of them assured Senator Smollet that the report of the impeachment panel would be rejected by the National Assembly when the report was debated later.

It was a beaming Smollet that later drove to the villa to inform the President of his breakthrough.

"Are you sure this will work?" Ambrose Oneya asked as they both settled down to watch the ZAT Television Network news later in the evening.

"It will, Your Excellency; I told you that those chaps have their price. They were just proving unnecessarily difficult and, uh! …"

Suddenly, Senator Smollet became incoherent.

In fact, he felt like fainting, for at that moment he saw himself on the national network news of the private television station as he was passing the bribe of 20 million dollars to the Legislators while the newscaster announced the addition of the offence of perverting the course of justice to the President's long list of impeachable offences.

"You fool, you idiot, you brainless fool, you fell into a trap; now I am done for!" was all President Oneya could say as he stared at the television screen.

www.ingramcontent.com/pod-product-compliance
Lightning Source LLC
Chambersburg PA
CBHW072334300426
44109CB00042B/1432